The Intentional Student

17 Strategies

To Survive & Thrive In College

From Day 1

Patrick Phillips, MSW

The Intentional Student:

17 Strategies

To Survive & Thrive in College

From Day 1

MrPhillipsTheChangeAgent@gmail.com

ISBN-10: 0-9893739-4-0

ISBN-13: 978-0-9893739-4-4

Library of Congress Control Number: 2016915520

Published by: Educational Empowerment Group, LLC

First Edition

Dedication

This book is dedicated to college students everywhere. Though the college journey may seem daunting and challenging at times, you should remember that growth occurs when you step out of your comfort zones. Stay the course, be intentional about your educational experience, and you can succeed.

Contents

Dedication

Phase One: The Prerequisites

Chapter

Phase Two: The Process

Chapter

Phase Three: The Exodus

Chapter

the prerequisites

Chapter 1

Be Real with Yourself

You are at your high school graduation, in line with the rest of the graduates. You hear your name. You begin to walk across the stage, thinking about how much you had to overcome to get to this point. Even though an announcement was made that those individuals in attendance should not cheer or otherwise interrupt the flow of the graduation program, you hear your family screaming your name. One of your family members even brought a small air horn. At the conclusion of the ceremony, you are showered with hugs, gifts, and balloons. Your grandmother gives you a big hug and tells you how proud of you she is. Your parents are beaming with pride and joy. Your whole family takes you to dinner, and you think, *This is the best day of my life!*

As the day concludes, you go home, grab your phone and video message some friends about the day. As you lie on your bed, you begin to think, *What's next?* You were accepted into four colleges, but you do not know which one to attend. You are even a little afraid; you question whether or not you are even ready for college.

9

I want you to understand that being nervous about college is perfectly normal. Many perspective college students face some type of fear about attending college. Perhaps you are experiencing

YOU DON'T HAVE TO BE GREAT TO GET STARTED BUT YOU DO HAVE TO GET STARTED TO BE GREAT!!

some fears of your own as you move towards a postsecondary education. I certainly did. From personal experience, I felt that attending school in South Central Los Angeles and other surrounding low-social-economic communities put me at a disadvantage and I began to doubt myself. I started to feel inferior to those students who went to schools in better areas, lived in nicer neighborhoods, or were raised in two-parent households. All I could think about was all the advantages these kids may have had that I didn't. Maybe they were exposed to things I was not, they may have had private tutoring and additional prep classes. These were some of the fears that I faced that had a negative impact on how I viewed myself as a perspective college student. I wondered if my academic preparation had put me in position to be a successful college student. I was fearful about my ability to thrive. Who knows how many of these factors influenced my decision to skip going to any of the four-year universities I was accepted into. Instead, I chose to attend a junior college.

I know many of you are thinking, "You did what? Why would you turn down a four-year university to attend a junior college?" I am *not* saying there is anything wrong with attending a junior college, but the reason that I decided to attend was not a good reason: I was afraid to get out of my comfort zone.

I was stuck in a fixed mindset versus a growth mindset. Fortunately, I was able to recover; I eventually graduated from the junior college with an associate's degree and later transferred to Georgia State University, where I obtained a bachelor's and master's degree in social work. Furthermore, I was recently accepted into a doctoral program, which means in a few years, I will receive my doctoral degree.

As a new college student, it is not uncommon to have uncertainty and questions.

- Am I ready?

- Will I fit in?

- What classes should I take?

• What major should I choose?

• Can I live on my own without my parent(s)?

The answers to each of these questions will take care of themselves, assuming you answer this next question correctly: What is your "*Why*", for attending college? Your "Why", is your compelling reason for wanting to attend college.

Again, I know some of you are thinking, "What a stupid question." The truth is that this is probably the most important question to ask yourself, because your long-term success depends on your answer.

Students who have compelling reasons for going to college fare much better than students who are going for the wrong reasons:

• Your friends are going.

• It sounds cool to be a college student.

• You want to make a lot of money.

• Your parent(s) told you that you will have to move out or get a job if you do not attend college.

Becoming a college graduate is a marathon, not a sprint. You will face adversity throughout, including the need to conquer challenges with your studies and money and transportation issues. You must keep your grades up at all times or risk being ejected from the program. Some grad students get derailed by life events, such as a relative getting sick, the loss of a relationship, or the fact that you are now at a point in your life that you have to make everyday decisions for yourself independently.

I faced all these challenges at different points in my college career, but probably the toughest was when I lost my employment while obtaining my master's degree. During this period in my college career, I had a twenty-hour-a-week internship; I was taking seventeen units a semester *and* working a job on graveyard shift. After I lost my job, I tried to find another graveyard shift position so that my school and internship schedule would not be impacted. I was unable to find another graveyard shift position. For several months, I struggled while stretching my financial aid checks, and enjoyed the delicacies of top ramen. I was barely able to pay my bills. Things got so tough that on some days I could only put two dollars' worth of gas in my 1992 FAR 600rr motorcycle so I could drive to school, to my internship and back home. On a few occasions, my motorcycle cut off on the freeway while I was trying to make it to class. My saving grace was the Highway Emergency Response Operators (HERO), an Atlanta service-call program that helps move stalled vehicles off the road. The HERO driver put enough gas in my motorcycle that allowed me to travel two or three more days. I was determined to finish school and earn my degree. This is how I made it back and forth to school on many occasions during the last six months before graduating and earning my master's degree.

The point here is that if you do not have compelling reasons and know your *"Why"* for attending college, it will be difficult to push yourself to succeed when similar challenges arise (and they will). My *"Why"* for being in college—my desire to be one of the first in my immediate family to graduate college—helped me to persevere when it would have been easy to just quit!

In addition to having a purpose, a "Why" for being in college, students who perform best are those who have what many call a *growth mindset* versus those who have a *fixed mindset.* Individuals with a growth mindset view challenges and adversity as opportunities for growth. They look forward to and embrace challenges. It fuels them.

On the other hand, individuals with fixed mindsets run from challenges. They would rather remain as mediocre because it's safe. The fixed mindset says, "I would rather remain stagnant and safe and look good than be uncomfortable and struggle." Individuals with fixed mindsets view failures as embarrassing character flaws. In comparison, those with a growth mindsets view failures as opportunities to learn and do better.

There are times you will have a rough day. There is a quote by Les Brown that really motivates me: "Don't say I am having a bad day—say I am having a character-building day."

You see, there are two completely different mindsets to the same challenge. Let's do some activities to help you discover your purpose your "*Why*" for attending college and help you figure out if you have a fixed or a growth mindset.

Fixed Mindset	Growth Mindset
Avoids challenges	Welcomes challenges
Feels that challenges are failure that expose personal weakness	Perseveres through obstacles and believes that challenges are opportunities for personal growth
Feels threatened by the success of others	Supports the efforts of others to succeed as well
Avoids and/or ignores constructive criticism	Seeks out and embraces constructive criticism

Activity: Growth or Fixed Mindset

Do you agree or disagree with this statement: "You have a certain amount of intelligence and you really can't do much to change it." Explain your answer.

_____

_____

_____

Explain in detail, your "Why" for attending a post secondary institution? How will obtaining a degree (s) help you fulfill your goals?

_____

_____

_____

It is said that the process is more important than the product. What does this mean to you? Do you agree? Explain your answer.

_____

_____

_____

When you reflect on recent decisions made during a challenging situation, would you describe your mindset as a growth or fixed mindset? How did your mindset impact your decision?

_____

_____

_____

_____

_____

List three of your areas of strength (existing abilities) and three areas of weakness (areas for growth). What are some strategies you can implement to improve the growth areas you listed?

_____

_____

_____

_____

_____

_____

Chapter 2

The Unintentional Student

If someone goes to class but does not show up mentally, did he really attend class? If someone is enrolled in school but does not do the work, is she really a student? The student who enrolls in school, attends classes each day, and completes the assignments is intentional about being a college student.

The difference between the above-mentioned students is intentionality or lack thereof. As a college instructor, this lack of commitment or purpose boggles my mind. I don't understand why students enroll in school but are not intentional about anything they do academically. They show up to class late, they do not read the textbook before class, they ask for extensions because their work is late, they write their essays minutes before they are due, they don't participate in class, they spend more time on social media than on their coursework—and they somehow expect good grades.

I once had a student who was dropped from my online course during the no-show period. This person then asked to be reinstated.

As usual, I began to conduct research to see *why* the student was dropped, and I discovered something very interesting. Because the course was an online class, the only way that I can determine whether or not a student is attending or actively participating is if they complete the assignments in queue. When I began to check  my grade book, I noticed that this student had not completed any of the initial four assignments. I had to inform the student that I could not reinstate him because he was not attending the class or participating in any way. I had to explain that reinstating him would put him in a situation in which it would have been difficult for him to recover because he had failed to complete any of the assignments. What was most interesting was that the student became upset and had a confused look on his face. He just didn't understand why I was not able to reinstate him.

Students need to be aware that lack of participation soon becomes a lack of progress. The inability to adapt to what is expected of students at the level of post secondary education not only leads to lack of success in the classroom, it can also contribute to lack of success in future endeavors beyond the classroom. When you fall short of an assignment or a grade that is borderline passing, your poor work efforts or habits can make it difficult to get that second chance or reconsideration from an instructor. Be intentional about the adoption of good practices and habits that can become a part of your identity as a student, one who strives to meet the expectations of the college regimen.

There was a time when I was an unintentional student, but I didn't know it at the time. I didn't realize this until I graduated with my associate's degree and moved to Atlanta and began taking coursework at Georgia State University. My grade point average (GPA) while obtaining my associate's degree was a 2.8; I thought I was really achieving something. People congratulated me, and I felt like I had really given my all. However, after I obtained my undergraduate and graduate degree with a 3.7 GPA, I realized that I truly had not given my all while attending junior college.

- Did I become a great student overnight?

- Did I become smarter because I moved to Georgia?

•Was there something special in the Atlanta water?

The answer to all these questions is *of course not.*

The reason I became a better student when I moved to Atlanta is simple: *I had no safety net; it was either sink or swim.* Because I was alone, I had no mother I could run to if things were not going well; no friends to borrow money from if I did not manage my money correctly; no grandmother to make me a hot plate if my refrigerator was empty. I had no one to depend on but myself. I had to quickly become very intentional about everything I was doing that involved my work and school. Like most people, I had the next level in me the whole time, and I just needed to tap into it.

Let's reflect for a moment: think about the first date you had with someone you really wanted to impress. Think about what you did to prepare to meet with them. Recall how you compared several outfits before choosing one. Reflect on how you color coordinated your belt and shoes or your purse and shoes. Think about how you sprayed on your favorite cologne or perfume to get your date's attention. Remember how you cleaned your car? Think about how you tidied up your house in case the date "went well."

Think about the intentionality surrounding the date. Because you wanted to impress your date, you made sure all the bases were covered. You did what you needed to do to ensure that there was no room for error, right?

Why is it that some people do not have this same level of intentionality when it relates to their education, schoolwork, and career? This is the level of intentionality and attention to detail needed to not only survive but thrive as a successful college student. Think about it:

•How much more successful could you be if you were intentional about your day?

•How much closer would you be toward achieving self-actualization if you gave 100 percent each day?

•How different would the world be if Martin Luther King Jr., Mahatma Gandhi, Helen Keller, Nelson Mandela, Malcolm X, or Henry Ford were not intentional about their business and contributions? Intentionality is everything.

>The Essence of Being an Intentional Student

One of the first strategies you can implement to be more

intentional is to simply show up with a plan. Map out your day:

- How much time will you spend in class?

- What will you do when class is over?

- How much time will you spend in the library?

- When will you eat?

- How long will you eat?

- How many breaks will you take?

- How long will it take you to commute to work?

As you begin to become more conscious about your process for academic success, you will find that being intentional requires that you be detail-oriented and give attention to your schedules and any details to make it work. There is an idiom that fits here: "The devil is in the details." This means that most of the time, it is not the large things that take us down; it's the accumulation of all the small details we did not do. Get a planner, and refer to it daily.

Another aspect of being the essence of intentional is cutting the fat. Have you ever eaten a piece of meat that had excess fat on it? What did you do in that situation? Most likely, you cut the fat off and discarded it. The same applies to your time as a college student and in life; you must trim away things that are in excess or that hold you back. More likely than not, you are going to have a few friends who elected not to attend college. You may have some who "attend" college but are not serious about being a student. As a result, they probably have more free time than you. They may ask you to hang out late during the week. They may want to have long, drawn-out conversations with you by phone. They may expect to chat for hours on social media. They think they are being your friend by spending time with you, but what they are really doing is absorbing valuable time away from your busy school schedule. They are getting in the way of your commitment to be being a successful student. Listen up: your friends may not have malicious intent, but it's important to set boundaries with people like this. Their bad habits and lack of intention can—and will—have a negative impact on you and your academic performance. Understand that I am not arguing that you cut everyone off, but you do need to be conscious of the fact that sometimes in life, some people can be liabilities that will hinder your development.

The unintentional student has a tendency to hang out on campus with no real purpose. These practices are not uncommon to witness. Every day, I see students sitting around campus, talking and just wasting time. They appear to be browsing and sharing social media platforms. While this conduct may seem harmless, it becomes problematic when the same students are engaging in this unproductive behavior hour after hour, day after day. The unproductive student literally spends hours daily being unintentional.

As an educator, what really frustrates me is that this type of conduct can continue, leading up to and during finals week. It is hard to imagine that students with this manner of practice do not have material they need to read or study. Interestingly, students who operate in this fashion will offer excuses, ask for extensions, and seem oblivious that they are not passing their classes or in danger of not meeting SAP (Satisfactory Academic Progress).

This brings me back to my opening query:

- If someone goes to class but does not show up mentally, did he really *attend* class?

- If someone is enrolled in school but does not do the work is she really a student?

Acquire people in your circle who will hold you accountable and hold you to certain standards:

- Ask each other to confirm when assignments are turned in.

- Offer to study together, either one on one or as a group.

- Remind each other of important dates and deadlines.

Don't sacrifice your future success by sacrificing your academic success now. Be intentional about your education!

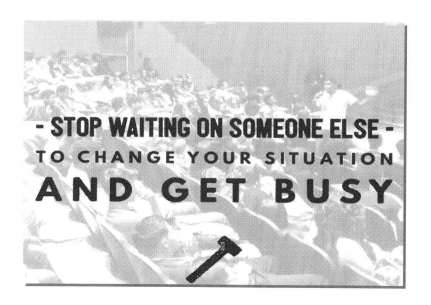

WAKE UP EVERYDAY WITH A PURPOSE AND INTENTIONALITY. SEIZE THE DAY!!

Activity: Are You an Intentional Student?

Create a chart similar to the one below and track your daily schedule in thirty-minute intervals for one week. After tracking your schedule for one week, what patterns do you observe?

- How much time do you spend studying?

- How many hours did you work on your job?

- How much time do you spend on social media?

- What adjustments in your daily schedule do you need to make to be a more intentional student?

Time	Activity (Examples)
6:00–6:30 a.m.	Wake up, shower
6:30–7:00 a.m.	Get dressed, check social media
7:00–7:30 a.m.	Check social media, watch TV, eat breakfast
7:30–8:00 a.m.	Ride bus to school (while studying)

After tracking your time for a week, what patterns do you see (studying, social media, sleep, eating, etc.)?

_____

_____

_____

After you have assessed the patterns, list the negative (*unproductive*) patterns you discovered. What adjustments need to be made to become more intentional (*productive*) about your education?

_____

_____

_____

One week later, write down your daily activities. Continue the schedule for one week. Compare your experience of with effectiveness (*productivity*) of an intentional week versus your previous non-intentional (*unproductive*) week.

_____

_____

_____

Do you notice a change in your productivity when you followed your intentional schedule? Explain.

Scavenger Hunt

Locate and visit the following offices, people, or departments on your school's campus and speak with some of the personnel regarding the services they offer.

✓ Library

✓ Reference librarian (inquire about online databases)

✓ Academic advisor

✓ Technology department

✓ Tutoring and enrichment services office

✓ Student activities department

✓ Financial aid office

✓ School police department

✓Department chair (for your major)

✓Disabilities services

✓Counseling department

Remember: A closed mouth does not get fed, so ask questions!
After visiting the above offices, people, or departments on your
school's campus, explain what is offered and how each department
can help you throughout the process as a college student.

_____

_____

_____

_____

_____

_____

_____

_____

Chapter 3

Choosing a Postsecondary Institution

Students use a variety of criteria when deciding what college to attend. Here are some reasons a student may choose a college:

- The school has a particularly prestigious academic program.

- The school won a recent NCAA sports championship.

- The student's parents are alumni of the school.

- The student wants to attend a school near the beach (or other desirable location).

- The student's favorite athlete went to the school.

The list goes on and on. While there is nothing wrong with using any of these as criteria for choosing a school of your choice, you must also consider a variety of other factors to ensure the postsecondary institution you choose is the correct (meaning the best) fit for you.

There are many different types of postsecondary institutions, including technical colleges, colleges, and universities. Before we address the differences between the various institutions, it is very important to note that no matter what college or university you choose to attend, you should confirm that it is fully accredited and the certifications and degrees they offer are valid and reputable. You can confirm that the school is accredited. To find out if an agency is legitimate, consult the Council for Higher Education Accreditation (CHEA), a private agency that accredits the accreditation agencies (www.chea.org). You can also check the US Department of Education (USDE) website at www.ed.gov for more information. Consult these agencies also to confirm if

some classes, if not all are transferable across public institutions, should you need to make a transfer at some point in your college career, this is important. With the increasing number of flexible academic programs online, a variety of nontraditional programs and schools have been created. Unfortunately, there are schools

that are only in the business of making money at the expense of students by providing them with illegitimate and worthless degrees. The impact of an illegitimate degree

or certification can have long-term impact, including financial strain and the inability to obtain employment. Generally speaking, most state and technical colleges are accredited, but you should do your homework before you apply. There are also many private colleges and universities that are accredited as well.

>Accreditation in the State of Georgia

The Southern Association of Colleges and Schools Commission on Colleges (SACS-COC) accredits colleges, technical colleges, and universities in Georgia and several other southern states including but not limited to Texas, Alabama, Louisiana, and Florida. Be certain that you are doing your research with the accrediting body for your region or country. Don't be afraid to ask questions. College is an important phase of your career and future.

"There are no foolish questions, and no man becomes a fool until he has stopped asking questions."

—Charles Proteus Steinmetz

>Articulation Agreements

You may be interested in finding out if the school you plan on attending has articulation agreements, officially approved agreements between two institutions. These agreements allow students to apply credits earned in specific programs at one institution toward advanced standing, entry, or transfer into a specific program at the other institution. This can be very beneficial because it may help you graduate sooner or increase your chances of getting into a specific program. For example, Atlanta Metro State College has an articulation agreement with Grady Hospital's radiology technology program. This articulation agreement not only aligns students at this college with Grady Hospital's radiology program requirements, but it also increases AMSC students' chances of getting into the hospital's program. Perform research to determine whether the program of study you are interested in has an articulation agreement with other schools or programs.

>Technical Colleges

Technical colleges are institutions that provide the "skills to pay the bills," so to speak. More precisely stated, technical colleges are known in academia as "work

IT IS GOOD FOR OUR SOUL TO CREATE WITH OUR HANDS

force-development" institutions. In general, technical colleges provide certification in a broad range of practical subjects, such as information technology, applied sciences, engineering, agriculture, and secretarial skills. Examples of programs of study may include certifications in areas such as HVAC (heating, ventilation, and air conditioning), cosmetology, barbering, graphic design, electrical, plumbing, and truck driving, to name a few. Upon completion, many technical college program certification programs allow individuals to immediately obtain employment in their field of study. Many technical colleges also offer associate degree programs as well. However, an associate's degree at a technical college may not carry as much weight as an associate's degree obtained at a traditional college.

Many people skip technical colleges, saying things like "that's not a real college" or "you can't make money graduating from a program like that." However, this is not necessarily true. For example, my barber, who owns multiple shops including one that has nearly thirty suites that makes over $150,000 a year. In addition to being a successful barber and entrepreneur, he passed his skill and business knowledge down to his son, who is a barber himself and cuts hair for celebrities in Atlanta. What is most interesting about my barber's son is that he is barely eighteen years old. This young man probably makes more than your average college graduate with a degree because he has mastered his skills in a demanding trade.

Moreover, I was recently reminded of how important skilled individuals are to society. I recall when the plumbing malfunctioned at my house. They replaced a portion of my plumbing, and it cost me nearly $2,000. What makes this story truly interesting is that they only worked for about three hours! In those three hours, the plumber made what it takes the average person weeks to make. I am sure they laughed all the way to the bank. If you have ever had your heat or air conditioning go out, you know how quickly you call an HVAC company to make the repair. No one wants to sit in a cold or hot house. We value our comfort.

The great thing about skills and trades is that in many instances the jobs cannot be outsourced, and the skills are transferable. If you know how to cut hair, you can go nearly anywhere in the world and cut hair. If you know how to wire electrical systems, you can work nearly anywhere in the world and work in a variety of industries. Some additional *advantages* of attending a technical college include coursework flexibility, the ability to obtain employment immediately following graduation, access to hands-on experience throughout training, lower cost of programs, and more. In addition, many programs are shorter than traditional college programs, and many states provide grants to attend technical colleges that are not based on income.

Some of the disadvantages of attending a technical college include the inability to earn a bachelor's degree; some of the classes you earn may not transfer to a college or university should you choose to attend at a later time. Furthermore, if you graduate and find there isn't a lot of demand in your chosen field, you don't have as many other skills to fall back on as you would with a broader education. Lastly, you may not be able to receive as large of a financial aid package as traditional college students.

>Colleges

Colleges are more challenging to define than universities and technical colleges because of the multitude and diversity of colleges and the type of programs they offer. There are some colleges that only offer certifications and associate degrees. Others offer certifications and both associate and undergraduate degrees (bachelor's). I obtained my associate's degree from a community college that only offered certifications and associate's degrees. However, in Georgia, we have several colleges (Morehouse College, Agnes Scott College, Atlanta Metropolitan State College, and Dalton State College, for example) which offer bachelor's degrees.

Generally speaking, colleges are what individuals in academia refer to as *teaching institutions*, as the majority of emphasis is on teaching. This is different from some institutions that are considered research institutions that focus on research and setting trends. Generally, research institutions are larger universities like Georgia Institute of Technology (GT), University of Georgia (UGA), and University of California Los Angeles (UCLA) to name a few.

Some of the advantages of attending a college include smaller class sizes and lower cost (if the school is a state college). In addition, you'll enjoy more individualized attention, and your instructors are more likely to know your name. At smaller schools, there is a greater likelihood that you will meet with your instructors (versus teacher's assistants). They may also accept students whom larger institutions may not have admitted. A smaller overall environment makes it more difficult to get lost in the shuffle. The degrees and units you take generally will be accepted at many other universities.

The fact that units are transferable is very beneficial. The ability to transfer credits/hours from a college to a university means that you can attend a college for two  years, obtain an associate's degree, and transfer to a university as a junior. The opportunity to transfer is great for several reasons. For one, attending a smaller environment first allows individuals to get acclimated to the college experience and learn what it takes to be a successful college student before going on to a larger university environment, which may be less forgiving. The second reason is that students can save a lot of money by initially attending a state college and later transferring to a university. Instead of paying expensive tuition at a university for four years, students can attend a college for two years and then transfer to a university. This strategy is also beneficial for students whose high school grades or test scores prevented them from initially attending a university.

>Access Colleges

Access colleges are institutions designed to help ensure that individuals have equal opportunity in education, regardless of their social class, gender, ethnicity, background, or physical and mental disabilities. There are several students at access colleges who are initially denied admission to larger higher-education institutions because they did not meet the requirements at the time. Some are able to transfer to the same institutions that initially denied them. Students are able to do this because while in school, they were able to raise their GPAs and otherwise fulfill requirements needed to attend the schools that initially denied them. Interestingly, some research shows that many students who take this route not only do as well as students who initially attend larger institutions, they also perform better in many areas.

I know that my decision to attend a college and obtain an associate's degree before attending a university was a great decision; it allowed me to get accustomed to the college experience and learn what it took to be successful in college. It also helped to build my confidence. In many ways, had I not obtained the solid foundation I received while obtaining my associate's degree, I would not be the person I am today—an author, speaker, college instructor, and inspirational speaker.

Some of the disadvantages of attending a college are that they may not have the name recognition of larger universities. Smaller schools can only offer limited majors or academic programs. Colleges may also have fewer amenities such as housing, recreational facilities, extracurricular activities, or student organizations. Most have smaller athletic programs.

>Universities

Universities are generally larger postsecondary institutions. The most obvious differentiators of universities and the previously mentioned postsecondary options are that universities focus on research and offer graduate degrees. This means that many universities not only have the ability to issue bachelor's degrees, they can also offer master's and even doctoral degrees. Like colleges, there are both private and public universities. Generally speaking, private colleges and universities are much more expensive than state colleges.

>Research Institutions vs. Teaching Institutions

Research institutions are schools that engage in extensive research activity; in the process; they also help to set trends. Research institutions do this by increasing the bank of knowledge available about the specific subject as well as broadening the possibilities of how to utilize that knowledge to society's best advantage. Many advances in medicine and technology have occurred at research universities throughout the world. Although the term *research* often implies natural-science research, there are also many research institutes in the social sciences as well, especially for sociological and historical research purposes. Students who attend research institutions increase their possibilities of being on the cutting edge of new technology, research, and discovery.

Some of the advantages of attending a university may include well-known faculty, a prestigious school name, having access to new research, state-of-the-art facilities for research publication, a larger range of disciplines taught, and contact with graduate students. Larger schools can also offer greater amenities, which may include enhanced student life, more extracurricular activities, larger alumni associations for networking, fraternities and sororities, and in some cases, more athletic programs.

Some of the disadvantages of attending a university may include a lack of personal attention due to larger class sizes, which can also result in reduced interaction between teachers and students. Universities may be more expensive. It may be easier for students to get distracted or feel "lost in the shuffle." As a result, students may experience reduced opportunities to build relationships with instructors.

Let's do a couple of activities that will help you in your process as you explore which sort of postsecondary institution you would like to attend and the best fit for you.

Activity: Finding The Right Fit (College/University)

What are the nonnegotiable conditions you are looking for in the college or university you plan on attending?

_____

_____

_____

What careers are you interested in pursuing?

_____

_____

_____

What type of education (certification or degree) is needed to reach this goal?

_____

_____

_____

What is your ultimate educational goal? Certification? Associate's? Bachelor's? Master's? Doctoral degree? Explain why.

_____

_____

_____

List five schools you are interested in attending.

_____

_____

_____

_____

_____

List the acceptance requirements of each postsecondary institution. (GPA, ACT and SAT scores, essay, etc.). You may need extra paper.

_____

_____

_____

_____

What agency accredits each of the five schools you are interested in attending? Is the accrediting agency legitimate and reputable?

_____

_____

_____

_____

Are you on track to get accepted in the postsecondary institutions you selected above? Do your GPA, SAT, and ACT scores meet their requirements? If not, list what you need to do to get on track.

_____

_____

_____

What is the cost of attendance for the five schools you selected?

_____

_____

_____

Which school has the most respected program in your intended field of study?

_____

_____

_____

If you are interested in attending a university, is it possible to attend a college first then transfer?

_____

_____

How does this information impact your decision on which school you want to attend?

_____

_____

_____

_____

_____

_____

_____

_____

_____

_____

_____

_____

_____

_____

ADVISORS
HELP YOU SET
YOUR SAIL IN

THE RIGHT
DIRECTION THEN HELP
YOU STAY ON

COURSE  

Chapter 4

I Don't Need to See an Advisor, Do I?

You've been accepted into the college of your choice, you've filled out your FAFSA (Free Application for Federal Student Aid) form, and now it's time to register for classes. Many students new to the college experience have a misconception that college is about taking the classes you want to take. While you will be able to choose many of your electives, this isn't necessarily true. Depending on your major, you will need to take a core group of classes. Many colleges now have Guided Pathways, a road map of

what classes to take semester by semester depending on your major. (See example below.) Many Guided Pathways allow students to decide how quickly they want to graduate. For example, if you want to graduate in four years, your Guided Pathway may require you to take fifteen to eighteen hours per semester. If, on the other hand, you want to graduate in six years, you will need to take nine to twelve units per semester. You will have to decide how heavy of a course load you can manage.

At this point, it's natural to have questions.

- How do I know which classes to take?

- What should my major be?

- What time of day should I take my classes?

- How do I balance my schedule?

The answer is simple: meet with an academic advisor at your school. "But won't my Guided Pathway cover all that?" you may ask. The answer? Yes—and no. There are a variety of factors to consider when registering for classes.

Checklist

(Information to Bring to Your Meeting with an Advisor)

✓ Work Schedule

✓ Guided Pathway

✓ Degree Audit

✓ Academic Transcript

✓ Idea of what classes you want to take

Multiple factors should be taken into consideration at this point:

- If you are not a morning person, you probably should not take classes early in the morning.

- If you work a night shift job, you probably should take classes late morning or in the afternoon. Otherwise you will have difficulty staying awake in class.

- If you have a busy schedule outside of school, you may want to take all your classes on two days to free yourself the rest of the week.

- If you do not have a vehicle, you will need to work around the limitations of public transportation schedules.

- If you have a commitment to pick up a child from school, you may want to consider a schedule that will allow for those situations.

Ultimately, you want to ensure your class schedule is structured so you can be a successful student.

As you can see, there is a lot to think about when deciding when and what classes to take, which is why you are encouraged to work with an academic advisor who can help you navigate the process.

If you are not strategic in your decisions now, you will only make things difficult for yourself. Consider what can happen if you are not strategic in choosing your class schedule. You may take classes at the wrong time of day, which can cause you to be late on a regular basis. Chronic tardiness will also impact your grades. If you take classes that are not relevant to your major, it will take you longer to graduate. You will also potentially waste money by increasing your student debt with no return on investment.

The most dangerous aspect students encounter by not being strategic when choosing their class schedule is jeopardizing their SAP (satisfactory academic progress), a requirement for continued financial aid. Getting low grades or having to withdraw from classes to avoid an F or D grade hurts you long term because it impacts your GPA (grade point average). If your GPA falls low enough, you could be placed on academic probation.

Can't commit to a major yet? That's fine; your academic advisor can help you register for general classes that can transfer to a variety of majors. This can help buy you time to decide what you want to major in.

To conclude this chapter, I want to

> **IF YOU FAIL TO PLAN, YOU PLAN TO FAIL**

share a true story that emphasizes the importance of working with an academic advisor. I knew of a student who had graduation invitations made and invited his family to his graduation ceremony —only to discover that he was not eligible to graduate! He was using one course to fulfill two obligations and had a D in a course that required a C for his major. Consequently, not only did the student have to deal with the disappointment of not graduating, but he also endured the embarrassment of inviting his family to a graduation ceremony he could not participate in. This student could have possibly graduated on time had he visited an academic advisor earlier and made the necessary adjustments to save himself the embarrassment of not being able to participate in his ceremony.

Let's complete a few activities that will help you prepare to register for classes.

Activity: I Don't Need to See an Advisor, Do I?

What careers are you interested in pursuing upon graduation? What major will fulfill your objective?

_____

_____

_____

Who is the academic advisor at your school? Use the space below to record their name, office location, office hours, phone number, and e-mail. (Remember to bring a copy of your Guided Pathway form with you to this meeting!)

_____

_____

_____

What is your employment schedule? If you do not have one yet, what do you anticipate it being during the semester?

_____

_____

_____

How do you need to plan your work, school, and study schedule to make your education a priority?

_____

_____

_____

Do you need to make any adjustments to your work schedule to ensure your academics are a priority? If so, detail them below:

_____

_____

_____

After analyzing your Guided Pathway, what have you discovered about how the classes are distributed each semester?

_____

_____

_____

If your core class selections are all difficult, have you selected some electives to balance the challenging classes?

_____

_____

_____

How many credit hours/units will you take per semester?

_____

What is your timeframe for graduating? How many credit hours/units will be required per semester to meet your timeframe? Do you feel this strategy is best for you to succeed? If so, why? If not, how can you improve it?

_____

_____

_____

Speak with your academic advisor regarding the course load you are able to handle considering your lifestyle.

The idea behind the guided pathway is to guide college students to complete a degree in a timely approach if they choose a program and develop an academic plan early on. The guided pathway provides a clear road map of the courses they need to take to complete a credential. Below is an example of how a guided pathway may be structured.

Year 1

		Fall Semester			Spring Semester		
	Course #	Course Name	Credit Hours	Course #	Course Name	Credit Hours	
Area A Essential Skills	Engl 1001	English Composition 1	3	Engl 1002	English Composition 2	3	
Area B Institutional Req	Amer Lit 1001	Thinking and Learning and Communication	4				Freshman Year Total Credit Hours
Area C Humanities and Art							
Area D Math Science				Biol 1106+ 1106 BLab or Chem 1212 + Clab 1212	Prin of Biol 1+Lab or Gen Chem 1+Lab	4	
Area E Social Sciences	Politics 1001 Economics 2104	Amer Gov Prin of MacroEcon	3 3	Hist 2011 or Hist 2012	U.S. Hist 1 or U.S. Hist II	3 3	
Area F Prog of Study				Economics 2105	Prin of Micro Econ	3	
Additional Requirements	Freshman Year Experience	FYEx 1740	*1				
		Total Hours	**13**		**Total Hours**	**13**	**26**

Year 2

		Fall Semester			Spring Semester		
	Course #	Course Name	Credit Hours	Course #	Course Name	Credit Hours	
Area A Essential Skills	xxxxxxx 1	xxxxxxx xxxxxxx 1	3	xxxxx xxxx xxx 2	xxxxxxxxxx xxxxxx 2	3	
Area B Institutional Req	xxxxxxxx	xxxxxxxxxn	4	XXXXXX XXXX	XXXXXXX XXXX	4	Sophomore Year Total Credit Hours
Area C Humanities and Art				XXXXXXX XXXXX X		3	
Area D Math Science	XXXXXXX XXX	XXXXXXX XXXXXXXX	4	xxxxx xxxx xxxxx xxx	xxxxx xxx xx xxxx xxxx		
Area E Social Sciences		xxxxxxx xxxxx or xxxxxx xxxs	3	xxxxxxx xxxx xxxxxxx xx	xxxxxx xxxxx xxx 2	3	
Area F Prog of Study				xxxxxxxxxx ssss			
Additional Requirements							
		Total Hours	**14**		**Total Hours**	**13**	**27**

Students who receive this guidance and support are more likely to stay on plan. Per the example above, upon successful completion of the course work the student would earn **53** related credit hours moving forward toward their credential.

IT'S NOT HOW MUCH YOU RECEIVE, IT'S HOW YOU SPEND IT.

Chapter 5

Give Me My Money (Financial Aid)

This may be some readers' favorite chapter. After all, we are talking about money—and who doesn't like to talk about money?

We are going to have some fun and explain why you should not spend your money frivolously if you get a financial aid disbursement after your classes are paid for. However, we must first cover some important foundational information.

Firstly, make sure you have completed your FAFSA form before the deadline. Deadline dates vary by school and state, so I recommend you communicate with the financial aid offices so you will know when your FAFSA is due.

What's a FAFSA? It's the free application you need to apply for the various student aid programs managed by the federal government. You can learn all about these programs at www.fafsa.ed.gov. The government analyzes the financial information you and your parent(s) submit, to determine your need for financial aid assistance to attend college. Generally speaking, the less money you or your family earn, the more likely you are to qualify for free financial aid assistance. The more money you or your family earn, the more likely you are to qualify for aid that you have to pay back. But let's talk about it in further detail. Remember, you should view the FAFSA website and your particular account for more details. The FAFSA office also has representatives you can speak with to get your questions answered. Also keep in mind there is a process called verification, in which your school's financial aid office may require you or your parent(s) to submit documentation that supports the financial information you provided in your FAFSA.

Finally, be aware there are fake websites that have web addresses similar to the federal FAFSA website. Do not provide these sites any personal information! Look for the (.gov) in the official website URL. https://fafsa.ed.**gov**

>**Different Types of Financial Aid**

Before we break down the differences in financial aid (including loans), let's first talk about a free, important option many people do not take advantage of. Not pursing this is one of the aspects I regret about my college experience. If you want free money, apply for grants and scholarships.

Grants and scholarships come from a variety of sources, including foundations, organizations, schools, and places of worship. If you visit your local bookstore, you will find dozens of books geared toward helping students discover and apply for grants and scholarships. Be prepared to complete essays as part of the application process for grants and scholarships.

An interesting component about scholarships and grants is that there are so many. They are available for individuals who meet all sorts of criteria, including (but scarcely limited to) being left-handed, having a great GPA, or being the first person in your family to attend college. Basically the options are unlimited, and I am sure there are scholarships you can qualify for. Take advantage of grant and scholarship opportunities! To learn more, speak to your high school counselor and the financial aid department at the college you want to attend.

Is it worth the hassle of applying for grants when you can just take out loans? The answer is unequivocally yes. Applying for grants and scholarships is worth the hassle because the money is free! Grants, like scholarships, are financial aid for college that does not have to be paid back. The major difference between the two is that grants are often need based, while scholarships may be either need or merit based. Athletic scholarships are merit based, meaning you have to have a strong academic record and special talents to be considered. You will not have to pay the money back.

Remember that poor academic performance can result in academic probation. If that happens, the funds will be placed on hold until your GPA has reached a satisfactory standard.

Here is a nice piece of information for you: after your classes are paid for, any money left over is yours to keep. This is a much better option than acquiring student loans.

>Federal Financial Aid

After you successfully complete your FAFSA, you will receive an

electronic or paper notice regarding your status. The notice will tell you if you have qualified for aid and the type and amount of aid you will receive. You may also have to elect that you accept the aid award amounts. There are two main types of aid; free financial aid and student loan financial aid. Furthermore, there are also two types of federal student loans, something we will discuss later in this chapter. The only requirement to continue to receive either or both is that you must maintain your SAP standards. In my opinion, the option you really want to focus on is the free financial aid because you do not have to pay the money back when you maintain your SAP. In order to maintain SAP and thereby protect your money, you must pass the majority of your classes and maintain the minimum GPA (as required by the federal government).

Remember, just because you have to maintain a minimum GPA does not mean the minimum is what you should strive for. Moreover; in addition to maintaining a minimum GPA, SAP has a second component: students must also pass a specific percentage of all classes taken. As it currently stands, the federal guidelines to maintain SAP are a minimum GPA of 2.0 and passing grades in at least 67 percent of all attempted hours. This means that you as a student cannot withdraw from too many classes, and you must also pass the majority of your classes. Students who do not meet these standards may be placed on academic probation and be ineligible to receive aid. While maintaining a 2.0 is the minimum standard, I recommend maintaining at least a 3.0 GPA to give yourself options, should you wish to attend graduate school at a later time. It is also important to be honest with the load of classes you can take per semester, to avoid low grades and unnecessary withdrawal of classes. Remember that requirements change, which is why I recommend you meet with your school's financial aid department yearly to stay abreast of any changes.

>Student Loans

As mentioned previously, student loans are a component of your financial aid options. In my opinion, student loans should be your last resort. I would try to obtain free financial aid before resorting to student loans. One key component to consider that make student loans

EXHAUST ALL MEASURES BEFORE USING STUDENT LOANS

a last resort is that you have to pay the money back. I know people who have over $150,000 in student loan debt—and their *minimum* payments are more than $800 a month. That's rent! When you combine paying this high student loan payment with other financial obligations such as child care, mortgage, car payment, groceries, utilities, gas, car insurance, and other day-to-day living expenses, you can see the importance of minimizing the amount of student loan debt you accumulate is imperative.

>Subsidized and Unsubsidized Loans

Subsidized loans are loans in which the interest on the loan is paid by the federal government *while you are a student.* This means that the interest is not increasing while you are still in school. With unsubsidized loans, the interest accrues even while you are a student. This means an unsubsidized loan costs more in the long term because what you owe grows even while you are a student. It is important to note that you can begin to pay the interest on an unsubsidized loan while you are in school to help reduce the overall cost of the loan.

There are two more aspects regarding student loans that we must discuss. If you must use student loans as an option to cover your academic expenses, I recommend only using federal student loans. I do not recommend taking out student loans from banks or other lending agencies. I say this because these lending institutions are not as flexible with payment options such as *forbearance* and *deferments* if needed, as federal student loans are. Forbearance and deferments allows you to temporarily postpone making your federal student loan payments or to temporarily reduce the amount you pay.

The final concern regarding student loans is that student loans never go away if you do not pay them! You cannot get rid of the debt in bankruptcy, and if you default on your payments, your wages and other income can be garnished. This debt stays with you forever until it is paid off or until you die. Try to avoid student loans, or if you must use them, borrow only what you need.

Write out a quick cost analysis to show the cost for you to attend college for one semester. Illustrate what amount of your financial aid award you will have left over and start thinking about budgeting.

Cost Analysis

Award amount per semester	Cost per credit/hour	Number of credits/hours you plan on taking	Student Fees
Total cost per semester including student fees	Book Expenses	Housing Expenses	What you have left over after expenses

Activity: Financial Aid

After receiving your FAFSA results, analyze the report. What type of aid are you receiving, free aid, student loans or other?

_____

_____

What amount are you being awarded?

_____

_____

Do you need to accept any of the amounts you are awarded?

_____

Does the amount you are receiving cover your tuition?

_____

_____

After your tuition and room and board are paid, what amount do you have left over? You are likely to receive this balance amount in a disbursement. How do you intend to use this money?

_____

_____

Chapter 6

Academic Professionalism

What you need to succeed in college can be summarized in two words: *academic professionalism.*

The best college students conduct themselves professionally and make their education a priority, not just something they get to when they have time. For example, have you ever visited a restaurant or business where the customer service was just horrible? Remember what you thought when you encountered representatives who were not knowledgeable about the products they were selling or took a long time to acknowledge your presence when you arrived. Say you ordered ice cream and they did not tell you the machine was broken or you experienced inconsistent quality among a company's many locations. It seemed as though not much effort went into providing excellent or good service, right? They did *just enough* to get by. I am sure you have had an experience similar to this at some point—just as I am sure that one of the first things that came to your mind was how *unprofessional* these people were, right?

Many college students make the mistake of making their education a side note in their lives, doing just enough to get by. What too many of these students do not realize is that their lack of academic professionalism will not only negatively impact their educational experience, it will also undermine their future as professionals.

>Show Up Every Time—and Show Up on Time

So how does a student show academic professionalism? The first component of academic professionalism is attendance. You cannot be a successful student if you do not attend class, show up on time, and remain for the entire class period. I have had students who miss half of the scheduled class meetings or leave early during every class meeting but somehow expect to pass. Interestingly enough, it is these same students who ask for extensions on their assignments and make excuses. I am sure the conduct mentioned above does not apply to you. But I would urge this type of student to consider the following list of questions:

- Would your place of employment allow you to stroll in for just half your shift? Would you expect them to also pay you for a full shift?

• Would your place of employment allow you to leave early all the time? And in turn, would you expect to get paid your entire salary?

• Would your employer accept excuses for your lack of commitment and failure to meet your obligation?

Even though most students acknowledge that their place of employment would not allow them this type of behavior, they still have difficulty transferring this same standard they have for their employment into the classroom.

>Don't Wait Until the Last Minute

During my initial year as a college instructor, I accepted student work in the same manner I did when teaching at the K–12 level. Everything came back to me on paper. As a result, I spent my first

- THE PURPOSE OF A -
COLLEGE EDUCATION
IS NOT SIMPLY
TO DO WORK,
BUT TO EXPAND AND
GROW AS AN INDIVIDUAL

year trying to keep up with hundreds of sheets of paper and having students fabricate stories of how they submitted their assignments (even though they had not). My second year as a college instructor, I decided to accept work in a digital format only via a system called Desire2Learn (D2L). D2L, which houses Dropbox at the institution, allows instructors to assign due dates and establish an end time for the assignments. Therefore, assignments can no longer be submitted after a certain date and time. This system not only allowed me to declutter my office, but it also presented a valuable opportunity to learn a lot about student work habits.

Because Drop box systematically logs the date and time when assignments are uploaded, I was then able to see how many of my students submitted their work literally minutes before the due date and time. Now, some readers may be asking why that mattered. "If they turned in their work," you might ask, "who cares when they did it, as long as it was submitted before the deadline?" That's a valid point, but let me share a conclusion I've reached as an instructor: when students submit their work that close to the deadline, chances are it's not quality work. The purpose of a college education is not simply to do work but to expand and grow as an individual. You simply cannot do this to your full capacity when your work is completed at the last minute. It is impossible to conduct research thoroughly, collect the information, interpret what you have read, and draft solid arguments that showcase your understating of the material when it is all done at the last minute. This is very important because it is within these processes that you experience an expansion of your knowledge base. When properly done, this is when growth occurs. When you do not go through the process, you will miss out on the opportunity for growth.

My favorite quote, by Oliver Wendell Holmes, states that "A man's mind, once stretched by a new idea, never regains its original dimensions."Envision a coach who makes his players run for extended periods of time or who makes them run scenarios in practice that can be more challenging than real game situations. Think about how coaches push their players to limits they did not think were possible. The coach does these things not to punish her players, but because she understands that it is only through challenge that her players develop to unimaginable levels, both mentally and physically.

Instructors do not assign work to simply assign work. They give assignments for the purpose of helping students grow into intellectual thinkers. However, this is not possible when a student disingenuously throws his work together and submits it at the last minute.

>Plagiarism

Plagiarism—taking someone else's work or ideas and passing it off as one's own—is a common problem in higher education. At many schools, submitting a previously used paper, purchasing someone else's paper online, or copying and pasting information from the

THERE ARE NO SHORTCUTS TO ANY PLACE WORTH GOING

Internet is grounds to not only receive an F, but for suspension or even expulsion as well. It is important that when you cite or reference information, you must give credit to the original author.

Many colleges now use software and programs that recognize plagiarism. While we will not conduct an English-language tutorial here, I want to provide a few strategies to help address plagiarism. When you want to use information from an original source, remember to synthesize the information and get a strong understanding of what the original document is stating. The next phase is not only putting the information in your own words but *making* the information yours.

I use the following analogy to help students understand how

important it is to make the information theirs and give credit where credit is due. When using another author's written original work, I have them think about it in this context: consider a music engineer who samples another artist's original compositions. When an engineer samples other artist's original work, they make changes and add their own contribution to the original composition; they may create a different melody by adding high or low pitch , or a combination of both by adding additional instruments; they may slow or speed up the tempo; and they may add some sound effects. When the engineer is done, the original composition still remains, but it has been altered dramatically to reflect the engineer's vision, to the point that it is now a new composition. This is an approach students can use when writing a paper, to avoid plagiarism.

You must read the information and have a clear understanding of its content. You can then take that information and make it your own through the proper process of analyzing it, interpreting it, adding your own views and opinions to it. In this manner, you are making new content that *is* your own. You have created a new piece of work. That said, after you have written your own version of the information, you must cite where you got the original information and give credit to the original author.

Most colleges have free tutoring services in which you can have your essays reviewed and edited; in addition, you can get help in a variety of other subjects such as math and science. I definitely recommend utilizing these supportive services; they are often included in your student fees.

>School Is Not the Club

Remember that the primary purpose of going to school, college, or any higher learning institution is *to learn*. While looking good and dressing confidently improves one's self-esteem, it is important to remember that college is a professional environment. Consequently, there are some dos and don'ts regarding your attire. Clothing that is revealing and exposes intimate parts of the body are not only inappropriate but distracting. Additionally, wearing hats in class, shirts, and pants with holes in them and saggin` exposing underwear are not appropriate. Someone once told me that when you step out of your house, you are auditioning and interviewing everywhere you go. What does the way you dress say about you?

Make a commitment to make your education a priority. Make a

statement with your attire that says, "I am about my business." There is a notable difference in students who consciously do this: they carry themselves more confidently, they engage the campus with a purpose, and they perform more effectively than those who do not exhibit academic professionalism.

Chapter 7

My Disbursement Has Arrived!

Many students have questions regarding how financial aid disbursements work. How it is calculated? How is the amount of money you receive determined? Generally, the money that remains on a student's account after classes, student fees, and housing (if appropriate) are paid for is disbursed to the student. For example, if your financial aid award allocated $7,000 per semester but your classes and student fees amounted to $4,000, you would then receive a disbursement in the amount of $3,000 (provided you have no other balances owed on your account). For many students, this is the most money they have ever had at one time. I implore you not to spend your money before you think strategically about it! I say this because this is typical behavior during the first few weeks of disbursement. You will see students walking around with new $300 headphones, $200 jeans, or $100 shoes. How do I know this, you may ask? I did it myself—during *my* uninformed years as a new, young student.

During the summer months leading up to the start of college, I purchased my first vehicle using my summer job earnings. One of the first things I did when I received my financial aid disbursement after purchasing my books was upgrade the sound system in my car. I purchased a set of twelve-inch subwoofers and two-thousand-watt amps, and I also replaced all the inside speakers in my car. I remember it to this day. I placed four six-by-nine-inch speakers on the interior of my car, along with sets of tweeters. If I tell you that people could hear my speakers down the block, it would be an understatement. I had one of the best car sound systems on campus; the treble was so clear and the bass was so deep that it rattled my trunk, and anyone riding in my car could feel the vibration in their chest. My friends and I used to have competitions to see whose beat was clearer and louder. Of course, I was the winner. Now when I reflect back, I can clearly see how loud speakers did nothing to help me as a student. Another one of my favorite quotes comes from Maya Angelou: "When you know better, you do better."

For some students, their financial aid disbursement may be their first experience with money management. Students, beware of the many mistakes that can be made with poor decisions and choices when spending unwisely on non-school-related items.

Take caution with spending that can take your focus away from planning and budgeting your funds on items of necessity. Mishandling of funds is common for new and young students. The number-one mistake young students tend to make is spending on expensive novelty items without first securing their education-related supplies such as books, technology, and other school-related materials. Be mindful not to put yourself in a position to have to make hasty last-minute purchases, like ordering books online in an effort to save money. When purchasing books online, pay close attention to delivery schedules. It won't matter how much you saved if the books arrive after the start of classes, will it?

When you receive your disbursement, stop and prioritize. Be strategic about spending. It is essential to remember there is a difference between *wants* and *needs*. No one *needs* $300 earphones; you can purchase a $40 pair, and they work just as well. No one *needs* $200 jeans; try purchasing a $50 pair instead. The average student does not *need* a $300 purse; consider purchasing a reasonably priced handbag. Think about it: purchasing expensive items generally means we are feeding our *wants*, not our *needs*.

I have a few suggestions for you to consider before spending your disbursement.

The first thing I recommend is to be frugal with your money.

"DO NOT SAVE WHAT IS LEFT AFTER SPENDING, BUT SPEND WHAT IS LEFT AFTER SAVING."
-WAREEN BUFFET

For example, if you need a laptop, purchase one—but don't buy the most expensive one. If you can get a laptop for $500, why buy a $2,000 one? There are also many proven strategies to save money on textbooks: purchase used textbooks, visit the bookstore early, buy digital copies of textbooks; or purchase them online before classes begin.

The second consideration to take into account is to save a percentage of your disbursement for emergencies. Your car may need repairs, your laptop might break down or get a virus, or any other sort of unexpected emergency can occur. It's best to be as prepared as possible, and that begins with having savings. Marshawn Lynch is a prime example of how saving money can provide flexibility and options. Lynch received a great deal of attention during his retirement announcement, but he received even more attention when sources announced that he has not spent any of the estimated fifty million dollars he earned while playing in the NFL. Lynch explained that rather than spend his NFL income, he lived off of the income he earned from endorsement deals with Pepsi, Nike, Skittles, and others. Consequently, Marshawn was able to retire at the early age of thirty in a league where athletes retire much older and with potentially permanent injuries. Marshawn understood that saving and having money for the long term was more important; he secured his future financially. I am sure with his millions, he could have purchased anything he wanted for short-term gratification, with little regard for what the future may hold for him. This is a lesson for us all. I encourage you to follow his lead. (To be fair, he did have millions to start, but you get the concept.)

The third piece of information I urge you to consider is to use your money on school-related expenses: books, paper, pencils, laptop, book bag, and transportation. I advocate wise spending because the money you receive from financial aid is awarded to you to support your academic journey. If you fail to have the supplies you need for classes and you do not perform well academically, you may be disqualified in the future from receiving aid. Therefore, it is very important that you take care of your academic expenses and necessities first.

Fourth, keep in mind that you may not want to disclose how large your disbursement is. That sort of disclosure opens up all sorts of problems for you, including the possibility that certain individuals will try to borrow money from you. For example, it is well documented that individuals who win the lottery often are targets for all sorts of money problems while attempting to help others who seek them out. Many times, they become broke or worse off than they were *before* winning the lottery. One of the main reasons lottery winners mismanage funds is that sometimes family and friends feel entitled to the winner's money. More often than not, the winner loans out or gives out more money than they should. Be on guard! Be cautious around individuals who feel a sense of entitlement to your educational disbursement funds.

>If Purchasing A Vehicle

There is nothing like the freedom of being able to come and go as you please. For many college students, obtaining a vehicle is a top priority. However, I have a few suggestions that may be beneficial to students considering the purchase of a vehicle. If you are interested in purchasing a vehicle and do not have stable employment, avoid financing. Remember that the main point of having a vehicle is to have transportation. Don't concern yourself with having the best-looking car in the parking lot. Instead of financing a vehicle, try purchasing a reliable used car for cash. Of course, you should always have it checked out by a mechanic before you purchase it to ensure you are not buying a lemon (junk) vehicle. There are services in which you can pay to have someone accompany you when you go to purchase a pre-owned vehicle, to safeguard you against purchasing a lemon (junk) car. This skilled person will look over the vehicle to make sure it is worth purchasing. Give yourself more financial flexibility by keeping your expenses low. Buy a vehicle you can afford. You really don't want to have your car repossessed because you chose to live above your means.

If you decide to become a vehicle owner, there are some responsibilities that come along with it. You will need at least the minimum level of liability car insurance (as determined by law in your state). You will need a school parking pass. As you begin to see, there are some important things that you will need to budget for when you have your own vehicle.

If you are thinking frugally, as I mentioned earlier in the text, that $2,000 laptop should be coming down to about $500 right about now. By purchasing a car for cash, you avoid having the monthly expense of a car note. That will make it easier to fund the other expenses that come along with owning your own vehicle.

It's also important to be practical as a young driver. Your insurance rates will be higher than those of older, more experienced drivers. If you do purchase a vehicle through financing, be aware that the newer and more expensive your vehicle is, the more your insurance will cost. You will also be required to have full-coverage insurance as opposed to the minimum liability insurance.

As a student, keep in perspective about *wants* versus *needs*. You have long-term goals; meet your current needs and consider allowing your short-term *wants* to wait.

Staying at Home

Have you considered attending a school that is near to home? If so, have you considered living at home while you are in school?

Using the chart below, you can explore the advantages and disadvantages of living at home while you attend school.

Pros of Staying Home	Cons of Staying Home

I know that college is a time of independence and making your mark in the world, but there are many benefits of continuing to live at home. You can save a lot of money this way, which you can use to purchase a vehicle, save to study abroad later, or move out and get your own apartment during your later years in college. You may have to continue to follow a few rules around the house, but it's much more economical (and it might even be free).

Lastly, be mindful of eating out too much or socializing above your means. Numerous students get themselves in debt trying to appear that they have more money than they do. Before you spend, you should always ask yourself: "Is this a want or a need?" Stay humble; you've got this.

YOU CANNOT KEEP OUT OF TROUBLE BY SPENDING MORE THAN YOUR INCOME.

Abraham Lincoln

Activity: My Disbursement Has Arrived

List some of the items you will need to purchase to support your educational endeavors. (e.g., books, paper, computer, etc.).

_____

_____

_____

_____

Identify the price of each item. Where can you get these items at the lowest cost? (The school bookstore may not always be the cheapest place to purchase your books or supplies.) Check out places like eBay, Amazon, Target, etc.

_____

_____

_____

Can you purchase used books? Can you rent books? Where can you locate used books?

_____

_____

_____

What do you plan to do with the money left over after you purchase school related materials? How much money do you plan to set aside in a savings account (emergency fund)?

_____

_____

_____

_____

_____

_____

Chapter 8

Building Rapport with Instructors

Some college students put their professors on such a high pedestal that they are afraid to communicate with them. This feeling can be further exacerbated when a student feels like he or she is just a number at a larger school. However, no matter the educational environment or how high the teacher-to-student ratio is, I want to stress to you it is very important to build student-teacher rapport. A good rapport provides a means for honest communication and mutual feedback. Some readers may be thinking, "Why do *I* need to have a rapport or a connection with my professor? Isn't their job to teach me and my job to learn?" But there are a variety of reasons to build a rapport with your professors.

Some of the most common reasons to build rapport include mentor opportunities, job placement, internship opportunities, letters of reference, and more. The fact is, many students learn better when they have a connection with their instructors. The need to build and maintain rapport can be summarized in this frequently used saying: "Your network equals your net worth."

Recently, I had to rely on my relationships with previous professors when applying to various doctoral programs. I asked several of my professors to complete a letter of reference for me, and boy, did they come through! Because of my rapport and

YOU CAN MAKE MORE FRIENDS IN TWO MONTHS BY BECOMING INTERESTED IN OTHER PEOPLE THAN YOU CAN IN TWO YEARS BY TRYING TO GET PEOPLE INTERESTED IN YOU.
Dale Carnegie

connection with them, the fact that we have maintained contact even after graduation, and because they are aware of the work that I do to promote the field of education through my work in the community, they were able to write favorable reference letters for me. These professors were able to complete references on my behalf that were unique and not "cookie cutter" or general.

You do not want to be the student who asks for a letter of reference when your professors do not know enough about you to complete one (or even worse, have no idea who you are). The experience would be like that of getting a referral from a friend who claims they have a connection somewhere, but when you arrive, the people there don't know who you are, and they don't know who your friend is either. Don't be a student who professors do not remember.

>Make an Impression

There are a variety of methods to build rapport with your professors. One of the simplest methods is attending class and being an active participant. There is a difference between *going to* class and *attending* class. I personally have had students come to class while on their phone and end the call right as they walk through the door saying, "I am going to call you right back." They then sit in class, aimlessly distracted on their phones using social media. Believe me, even if your professors appear as though they do not notice your lack of participation and engagement, they *are* keeping mental notes, and it can come back to haunt you when you ask for extra credit, an extension, or a letter of reference. Ask questions in class, participate in class discussions, complete your assignments on time, and complete the assigned reading before class. Instructors can't do their jobs if you don't do yours first.

Another strategy to help you stand out and build rapport with your professors is to show your enthusiasm for the course content by bringing current, relevant information about local events in to class for discussion. For example, say you are studying politics and there is relevant political news or a news article about local elections taking place. Trust me when I say that professors enjoy inquisitive students who bring real-life, relevant situations into the classroom for discussion.

The final two strategies are to complete your work to a high standard and meet with your professors during office hours for clarity on assignments when you lack understanding. For most instructors, outliers really stand out; instructors remember assignments that were completed to a high standard, as well as assignments that were completed with little effort and to poor standards. Instructors tend to not remember average work because it gets lost in the shuffle. I like the popular statement; I will see you at the top, because the bottom is too crowded. Ask yourself if you remember average people. Don't you tend to remember individuals who stood out in some form or fashion? I know I do. Be the student who completes assignments to a high standard. Your professors *will* take notice: "Wow, he put a lot of thought into this" or "That was an interesting perspective."

A final key strategy I suggest is to visit your professors during their office hours to get the answers to those pointed questions you did not get a chance to ask during class time.

You would be surprised at the number of professors who sit in their offices during office hours without a single visit from a student. You can use this time to get clarification on concepts and theories, ask about assignments, and talk about what you are learning in class and how it has been applicable outside the classroom. Make no mistake: *these are the engagements that get you noticed.* Your professor is much more likely to remember your name, who you are, and what kind of student you are if you take the time to invest in your own success. You did not hear this from me, but rapport with your professors can be the difference between an 89 percent in a class and a 90 percent when you are borderline and just a few points away. I don't know who said this, but there is quote I want you to remember: "A five-minute conversation with the right person can save you five years."

There are a multitude of good reasons for establishing a rapport with your instructors. I encourage you to take advantage of their expertise and experiences; it creates a mutual respect, trust, and a connection from which both the student and teacher can benefit.

Strategies to Build Student-Instructor Rapport

•Address instructors by the correct title.

•Come to class on time.

•To stand out, complete your work on time and to a high standard.

•Be an active participant in class.

•Visit your instructor during office hours to discuss the course content and related topics.

•Learn about your instructor's academic interest and speak with them regarding their interest.

•Keep conversations professional (no flirting).

•Never use profanity or inappropriate language in class.

•Be the student you would want in your class, if you were the instructor.

Activity: Build That Rapport

What are your instructors' office locations and office hours?

_____

_____

_____

How would you characterize your rapport with your instructors?

_____

_____

_____

How can you maintain or improve your student-instructor rapport?

_____

_____

_____

What are some of your instructors' interests in academia? What are their sports or music interests outside of academia?

_____

_____

_____

Have any of your professors published any articles? If so, what are they?

_____

_____

_____

Chapter 9
Communicating with Your Professors
(When there is an Issue)

While addressing this topic, we will discuss some of the inappropriate ways students approach their professors when there is an issue, as well as some appropriate ways to handle it. Some of the most common reasons students have disagreements with their instructors include a poor test grade or a lower-than-expected essay grade. When an instructor does not allow students to submit late work and an instructor makes an error in the grade book, conflict can arise. All of the above-mentioned issues are valid concerns to meet with an instructor and attempt to justify the disagreement. Students should consider that *how* you approach an instructor about a situation is key to getting the outcome you seek.

Recently, I was placed on a committee at a college with the task of creating eight videos to showcase some of the most common pitfalls college students encounter. I based one of the scripts on an actual situation in which a

Say what you mean, and mean what you say, but don't say it mean!

student approached an instructor after receiving a poor grade. During the incident, two instructors were sitting in the school cafeteria eating, when an upset student approached them about a grade they received on a paper. While this was an inappropriate time and place for such a discussion, the student's behavior only made it worse. The student slammed the paper down, nearly knocking their food off the table. The student then angrily began to explain how he could not understand why he received such a low score on the essay. Eventually, an instructor (who was not the student's professor) was able to calm the student down and explain to the student the proper way to address the issue.

For the record, this is definitely the wrong way to approach an instructor when you have an issue. Let's be honest—do you think the student received the outcome he was looking for?

If you were the instructor who was approached in such an inappropriate and disrespectful manner, would you make accommodations for the student, or would you stand your ground? Would you provide an opportunity for the student to resubmit the assignment, or would you let the grade stand? Keep in mind that your instructors are human beings with feelings and emotions. No matter how many degrees one may have or the number of professional accolades they have received, no one enjoys being disrespected, particularly in public.

>Addressing Your Issues

When you have an issue with an instructor, I recommend addressing it immediately during office hours, not during class. Do not wait weeks or until the end of the semester before addressing a grade or any relevant issue. Remember that you and your instructor are both adults, so be respectful and driven, with a satisfactory outcome in mind.

Things to Keep in Mind When Preparing to Meet with a Professor

✓ What are your professor's office hours?

✓ Consider face-to-face communication instead of e-mail.

✓ Know what you want to accomplish during the meeting with your professor before you speak to him or her.

✓ Make *requests,* not *demands*

✓ Thinking ahead: What are the possible alternatives?

✓ As the student, what are you willing to do to help the situation?

✓ What can you learn from the situation?

Try to reduce emotions during the conversation when discussing your concerns.

If you have questions regarding a particular test or paper, bring it with you, make it the focus of your conversation, and at some point during the meeting, ask what can you do to improve on future assignments.

Do not be afraid to ask for a second opportunity to submit your assignment. Some professors may provide second opportunities for students they feel deserve them. Always thank the professor for his or her time.

If after the conversation, you feel that discrepancies still exist, follow your school's policy to dispute a grade or file a grievance. You can generally find the complaint or grievance process in your student handbook or the school catalog. Your dean's office can also answer questions. Remember; file a grievance *only* if you feel it is truly necessary for a resolution. A grievance is generally defined as dissatisfaction that takes place when a student believes that any decision, act, or situation affecting him or her is illegal, unjust, or creates unnecessary hardship.

When it comes to assignments, take measures to ensure you are taking responsibility for what is required.

>What Not to Do When Meeting with Professors

You should never attempt to air grievances, concerns, or issues with your instructor during class or in front of other students. Bad timing can create a situation in which the professor may feel his or her authority is being undermined. It will be very difficult to get the results you are looking for by doing this. On the contrary, if you schedule a time to meet with your professor one on one, the professor may be able or willing to make accommodations that align with the integrity of the course and grading practices based on individual circumstances.

Do not speak to professors rudely or disrespectfully. Do not use profanity in your meeting. Do not make excuses to professors about why you did not submit an assignment. I have encountered a variety of creative excuses students use to cover for themselves regarding missed or late assignments: "I had a death in the family" or "The system would not let me

IT'S NOT WHAT YOU SAY IT'S *how you say it*

upload the assignment" or "You said the assignment was due on a different day." These are the types of excuses that make it difficult for instructors to give a student the benefit of the doubt when making a decision that can be crucial and may impact a student's academic standing.

Lastly, when communicating via e-mail, remove emotions from your text and keep it professional. DO NOT TYPE IN ALL CAPS TO LET INSTRUCTORS KNOW YOU ARE ANGRY! Always use the correct salutation (e.g., , Dr., Mr., Mrs., or Professor). Be sure to include a subject line, state the issue concisely, and add your name, course identification number, and the day you take the class with the instructor, so you can easily be identified. It can be time-consuming for an instructor to look through multiple class rolls to identify a student to determine which student sent the e-mail. Remember to keep all communication respectful and driven toward a satisfactory outcome.

Reflection: What is your take-a-way from Chapter 9?

THERE IS NO SUCH THING AS A PART-TIME STUDENT. IMMERSE YOURSELF IN THE EXPERIENCE OF BEING A COLLEGE STUDENT BY GETTING ACTIVE.

Chapter 10

The Parking Lot Student

The parking lot student is an interesting character. He is notorious for parking in the school parking lot, going to class, and then getting back in his car and going home. Now, some of you are thinking, "Isn't that what students are supposed to do? Come to school and go home?" but the answer is no. Research shows that students who spend more time on campus and involve themselves in constructive campus activities perform better and have a more holistic college experience.

I was once a student who could not wait to leave campus as soon as my classes were over, but after I started attending Georgia State University and the academic rigor increased, I soon learned the importance of taking advantage of the resources on campus.

It is important to understand that the research regarding student involvement and student success also refers to components of student involvement outside of academics such as visiting the school library or taking advantage of the academic support system.

One of the biggest regrets I have about my college experience is the fact that I had little involvement on campus outside of academics. I did not have a typical college experience because I had to work so much to support myself. I was what many would call a commuter student or parking lot student; I went to class, to the library, and back home. I never attended or participated in school events or school-related organizations such as student government, mentor programs, or fraternities.

Strategies to Help You Get Involved on Campus

✓ Join academic organizations on campus.

✓ Join nonacademic organizations.

✓ Join professional organizations.

✓ Attend conferences with school organizations.

✓ Start an organization on campus.

✓ Participate in school wide events (debate teams, homecoming, team games, movies, and more).

I am often reminded about my lack of campus involvement as it related to nonacademic activities when I engage in conversation with friends who talk about their fraternity line brothers and sisters, the trip they took with classmates, the random funny memories they created while hanging out on campus, or the awesome homecoming events they attended. One of my best friends' father  gave me advice years ago that I wished I had followed. He told me, "You will have your whole life to work and pay bills, Patrick. Enjoy your college experience." As I look back, I wish I had followed his advice because it was true. Find a healthy balance.

One of my favorite movies, *Avatar*, highlights the importance of balance. Finding a balance between academics and college activities can support students in getting the full college experience. Some of you may be thinking *Avatar? The movie with the big blue aliens living on Pandora?* Yes, that's the one. When

Jake, the main character, gets lost in the jungle, he is adopted by an alien tribe called the Na'vi. While living with the tribe, the Na'vi train Jake and show him their ways with the purpose of freeing him from his "madness"—the very human tendency to consume beyond one's needs. While learning from the Na'vi, Jake tried to learn the true meaning of "the people" and "seeing the forest." Jake struggled with the concept of seeing the forest because he was viewing the jungle on the surface level. What the Na'vi were trying to teach Jake was to embrace the value of everything in the environment: the sunlight, the natural world, the living animals, and the forest itself. The Na'vi wanted Jake to become one with the forest by immersing himself in the experience of being a Na'vi. The Na'vi believed there is a difference between being *in* the forest and being *one with* the forest.

The point here is that there is a difference between just *attending college* and *immersing yourself in the college experience*. Many colleges have organizations dedicated to supporting students throughout their college experience. For example, Brother 2 Brother is a support organization for male students. There is also another organization for female students called S.H.O.E.S. or Stepping High on Empowerment for Sisters. Both organizations meet regularly and provide opportunities for participants to network, attend conferences together, and support each other throughout their academic journeys. In addition to these two organizations, most institutions also have student government, science clubs, social science clubs, and a host of other student organizations that welcome new members.

Most colleges and universities have organizations similar to the ones mentioned above, though they may have different names. There are a number of clubs and organizations you can participate in based on your interest, to help support you as a student both academically and socially. Speak with your academic advisor or the student activities center to learn more about what your school has to offer. Take advantage of the organizations, clubs, and activities on campus, because your total college experience can be contingent upon your involvement to maximize your college experience.

Activity: Get Involved

What are your school's library hours? What resources does your library offer? Who is your school reference librarian?

_____

_____

What academic support groups or organizations are available on your campus (e.g., tutoring, study groups, disability services, etc.)?

_____

_____

Visit your school's student activities center, identify and list the student organizations and clubs available on your college campus (e.g., Brother 2 Brother, S.H.O.E.S., etc.). Are they coed?

_____

_____

_____

What organizations or clubs are you interested in joining? What value would you add to the organization?

_____

_____

_____

Attend a meeting of one of the organizations or clubs you listed above. What did you like about the organization?

_____

_____

_____

_____

_____

What are the benefits of joining the organization?

_____

_____

_____

_____

_____

What are the requirements to join the organization?

_____

_____

_____

_____

GOOD GRADES
DO NOT
HAPPEN
BY ACCIDENT.
....
THEY REQUIRE
INTENTIONALITY.
....

Chapter 11

Study, We're Talking about Studying

There is no substitute for hard work and discipline. Many people "should" themselves to death. How many times have we heard ourselves utter statements like:

- " I *should* go to the gym."

- "I *should* not be eating this so late."

- "I *should* be studying right now."

- "I *should* go to class."

- "I *should* wait before I purchase this."

It will be difficult to have the level of success you desire as a student, employee, or entrepreneur until your "I should" becomes your "I must."

To be a successful student, you must study, and do so regularly and consistently. It can't be something you do only when you are in the mood, something that you do not plan for, something you do only after you get your first F, or something you do the day before the midterm. You must be consistent or your grades will be nonexistent.

The number of students who go to see instructors two weeks before the end of a semester, pleading for extra credit or asking for the opportunity to complete an assignment that was due weeks ago can be disquieting. As an instructor, my thought process is always, *Where have you been?* When a student neglectfully delays with their course work and later seeks additional consideration, I am reminded of someone who buys flowers only when their significant other is mad at them or wants to break up with them. Why wait until matters are in dire need of attention to get active? Students, do not wait until you have a failing grade to be proactive. Be intentional about every aspect of your education.

>Find a Study Location

Before you attempt to develop a strategy for studying, you must first determine where you study most effectively. For example, some students study and work more effectively away from home.

Consider locations away from home such as a library, coffee shop, or bookstore. Which allows you to be much more productive? These away locations can free you up from a number of the comforts of home that can distract you such as television, siblings, a family dog, or dishes that may need your attention.

These are all diversions that can cause you to lag on your schoolwork.

While some students may feel comfortable studying at home, it may be difficult to focus if there are younger children around. Devise a plan that will support you in your effort to study at home.

Be honest with yourself and decide in what type of study settings you are most effective. While you may want to study in your dorm, it may not be the best location if your roommate always has company. Consequently, I recommend setting aside specific times daily to study in a library, bookstore, or coffee shop. In addition to helping you reduce distractions, an added bonus is that many locations provide free Wi-Fi or Internet access. You can use this resource to help you locate articles, perform research, complete discussions, and post and submit assignments online. This is especially helpful to students who may not have access to Internet at their homes. Remember to be specific and consistent about your study time; set aside blocks of time daily where you do nothing but study and complete assignments without distraction. And speaking of distractions…

>Reducing Distractions

One of the keys to a successful study session is reducing distractions while studying. The greatest distracter preventing many students from having a successful study session is the cell phone. With the constant social media updates, text messaging, and phone calls, your phone

study
(verb)
The act of texting, eating and watching TV with an open textbook nearby.

can keep you focused on everything *but* what you should be focusing on during study time. While social media is a valuable tool, it can impact your productivity when you sit down to work on tasks. It is not uncommon for students to allocate a specific amount of time to study in the library, only to shortchange themselves by spending countless minutes responding to their cell phones.

Because cell phones serve a multitude of purposes, we cannot simply just get rid of them or turn them off to reduce distractions. When studying, I recommend that you place your phone on airplane mode or the setting in which only specific, important contacts (for example, your children or caretakers) can call you while you are studying. This way, you can maximize your study time and reduce distractions. Additionally, you can log out of your social media profiles so you do not receive notifications while you are studying. Another great strategy to reduce distractions while studying at home is to place your cell phone in a different room than the one you are studying in. This way, you will not be distracted by every notification that hits your phone.

>Study Groups

Another effective strategy to help elevate your learning to the next level is to utilize study groups and work with collaborative groups. There are many reasons I support study groups. While working in groups, individuals can share their understanding of content, exchange ideas, and even divide tasks for various projects and assignments. However, a key factor when assembling study groups is choosing the right members for the group. You want to choose individuals who are consistent, hard-working, disciplined, and focused. To put it simply, choose group members who are as intentional about their education and coursework as you are—or even more. You do not want to choose the class clown or someone who is not serious about the business of being a college student; these types of individuals will be a distraction. The other aspect you must assess before deciding on study group members is fit and personality that match up with the tasks you are trying to accomplish. Some individuals are more laid back, others are more authoritarian. There are others who may be followers. Try to avoid situations in which personalities and work ethics may not complement your work ethics and efforts.

Types of Students in Group Projects
The Invisible Student rarely shows up to class and group meetings. They do not respond to group messages or e-mails.
What to Do: As a group, address the person if things do not improve, and if necessary, speak with your instructor about having the student removed from your group.
The Silent Student attends group meetings but does not participate. They rarely make recommendations or have an opinion about what should be done.
What to Do: Go around the group and ask each member to contribute. To help them feel safe and confident, be sure to ask direct questions and remain positive.
The Procrastinator takes on group tasks but never fulfills their portion of the assignment until the very last minute, causing the whole group stress.
What to Do: Create group deadlines and speak with all group

members about sticking to the deadlines agreed upon by the group.

The Over-Promiser and Under-Deliverer makes promises to take on many tasks but regularly fails to complete them. They always "have a connection" or know someone who can "do something," but they don't come through.

What to Do: As a group leader, make sure you collaborate and see everyone's work before the presentation, to ensure everyone had fulfilled their obligations. Provide constructive criticism in a supportive manner if necessary.

The Control Freak is very concerned about the project and often tries to take the lead by giving orders.

What to Do: Let them know you are capable and just as concerned with the assignment and will fulfill your obligations concerning the project.

Activity: We're Talking About Studying!

What time of day and what location do you feel you can be most productive with studying? Explain.

_____

_____

_____

Describe your study routine in detail (location, time, who is around, etc.).

_____

_____

_____

What distractions do you encounter when studying?

_____

_____

_____

What do you notice about your study routine that supports an effective study session?

_____

_____

_____

What do you notice about your study routine that hinders you from having an effective study session?

_____

_____

_____

_____

What strategies can you implement to address any distractions?

_____

_____

_____

_____

What changes can you implement to make your study sessions more effective?

_____

_____

_____

_____

IT'S NOT ABOUT

HOW MUCH
YOU WRITE,
IT'S ABOUT HOW
MUCH YOU RETAIN.

Chapter 12

You Write Too Much!

One of the major differences between college and high school is that the primary responsibility for learning is now on you. From my experience as an educator who has taught at the elementary, middle, and high-school levels, if a student did not pass the end of course standardized test, the *teacher* was held accountable. Teachers are asked why the student did not pass, why there was no "growth," and what *they* were going to do next school year to ensure that the student improved in the various areas. Teachers were also asked what differentiation of instruction strategies were used to ensure all learning styles were addressed, as well as what thinking maps were used to help the students understand the concepts being taught. Examples of these strategies included graphic organizers, OWL charts, ability grouping, having multiple ways to teach and complete assignments, and the list goes on.

As you can see above, K–12 educators take the brunt of the responsibility for lack of student success. Have no doubt that in college, this accountability shifts exclusively to you, the student.

No one is going to ask your college instructor why you received a D on an assessment or failed a course—*except you.* Your parent cannot come to the college and argue a grade or ask for extra credit on your behalf. If you are going to be successful, you are going to have to learn how to take notes, study effectively, identify and use your learning preferences, and compensate for instructors who do not teach to your learning preferences or style.

>Importance of Taking Notes

If you do not take legible, concise, and well-organized notes during class, it is going to be difficult for you to study, comprehend, and learn the material. One of the most common note-taking errors college students make is to try to write down everything the professor says. There are students who literally try to copy down an entire PowerPoint instead of summarizing and paraphrasing information and using graphic organizers.

This type of student will say things like, "Can you go back to the previous slide?" or "You are moving too fast" or even worse, "Can you provide us with the PowerPoint presentation?" The problem with the strategy of trying to write down everything is that you are not interpreting, synthesizing, and making the information yours. You are just copying information, which does not help you recall the information at a later time.

>Organizing Your Notes

I am sure some of you have watched the movie *Limitless*. The main character stumbles across a pill that allows him to access nearly every area of his brain. Because of this ability to use additional areas of his brain, the main character was able to learn new languages in hours. He could also identify and solve complicated patterns. This ability allowed him to manipulate the stock market and learn a variety of other skills in minutes. While there is no magic pill to help you learn and recall, you can identify patterns, organize your thoughts and notes, and study strategically so you can demonstrate at a high level what you have learned.

Teachers at the primary education level regularly use thinking maps or graphic organizers to help students learn concepts. Chances are that you have used them as well (Cornell Notes, Venn diagram, KWL chart, and other cause-and-effect charts, etc.). Interestingly, I rarely see college students using these types of graphic organizers to help them take notes, organize their papers, or study. Instead students just write notes in paragraph form without using tools to help them make connections in the information.

Use Google to search for *thinking maps* or *graphic organizers*. You can then print free sheets to help you organize your notes in class.

Examples of Graphic Organizers

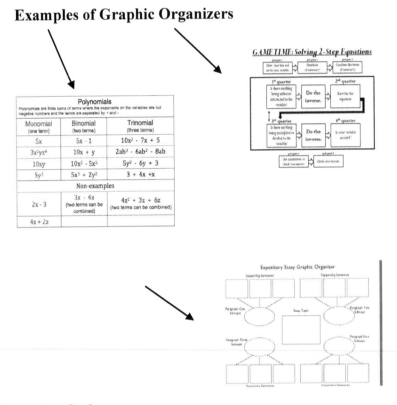

>Learning Styles

Learning style—an individual's unique method to learning based on strengths, weaknesses, and preferences—has received much discussion recently. Some professionals do not believe the research supports continued use or teaching learning styles. However, many schools and organizations continue to use learning styles to assist students academically.

Therefore, I will include some information regarding one of the most commonly used learning styles: the VARK (Visual, Auditory, Read/Write, and Kinesthetic) sensory modalities that are used for learning information. Perform a quick Google search to locate free VARK assessments that you can take to discover your learning style(s). It is important to note that many individuals learn by a combination of two modalities or methods.

For example, some students are kinesthetic and visual learners. Kinesthetic learning style means a student learns by doing physical activities (hands on) as opposed to listening to a lecture or watching a demonstration. A visual learning style is when a student learns the information by associating images and techniques.

Your college career counseling office should have access to the popular learning styles and personality type surveys to aid you in determining your learning style.

>Learning Style Definitions

•Visual learners prefer the use of images, maps, and graphic organizers to access and understand information.

•Auditory learners learn best by listening, as in speaking situations such as lectures and group discussions.

•Read/Write learners learn best through the use of the written word and taking numerous notes.

•Kinesthetic learners are hands-on learners who learn best through tactile representations of information (physical activities).

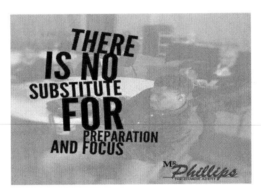

Learning Style(s) Reflection

Speak with your college counselor or career center staff about learning styles and/or the Paragon Learning Style Inventory (PLSI).

Activity: What did you learn about your learning style?

_____

_____

_____

_____

Do you consider yourself more of a visual, auditory, read/write, or a kinesthetic/tactile learner? Which learning strategies have you tried? Which is the best fit to your learning style?

_____

_____

_____

_____

Which learning strategy/technique will you try next semester, if you feel you need to make an adjustment?

_____

_____

_____

_____

SUCCESS AND FAILURES ARE THE ACCUMULATION OF THE SMALL THINGS THAT WE DO AND DO NOT DO.

Chapter 13

That Won't Happen to Me

Before we graduate to the Exodus section of our reading, it is imperative that we discuss some common issues outside of academics that can derail many college students. One of the most common stumbling blocks is the tendency for some students to allow their social lives to overshadow their academic lives. This was the case for Tim, one of my best friends in high school and college. In high school, Tim and I were a tag team of class clowns. We used to have the entire class laughing and distracted. If Tim was absent, I would make up for his lack of presence by really (*going in'*) straight clowning. We were such a duo that when my mother was asked to attend my parent/teacher conference regarding my behavior in class, she asked me to introduce her to Tim. She felt she needed to meet this person with whom I had such a camaraderie and bond that caused such disruptive behavior in class.

After I graduated from community college, Tim and I eventually met up at the same university. I noticed how quickly Tim had climbed the social hierarchy at the university; he was in a fraternity, he attended all the parties, and he was even building a reputation for himself at the college. Unfortunately, the heavy partying and social life ended his college career. Even worse, Tim also struggled with alcoholism and drug addiction. It has been more than ten years, and Tim still hasn't fully recovered. Occasionally, I check in on him via social media, but he is not the same person he was before becoming a victim of his social life.

Take a moment to learn from Tim's example. You should have the presence of mind to find a healthy balance between your social life and your academic life. Your future depends on it.

Another common occurrence that impacts student academics and even causes some students to drop out is unplanned pregnancy. As a professor, speaker, and community activist, I often have a conversation with young adults about the importance of acting responsibly when engaging in sexual activity. Inevitably, I always get the same response: "That's not going to be me" or "I am not going to get caught up." My reply is always, "Don't say not me." I make this statement to young adults because I want them to realize just how easily it could be them if they are not taking the appropriate measures to not get pregnant or to father a child. Why not you?

I recall a difficult conversation I had with a young man regarding this same topic. As we conversed, he informed me that he had impregnated two young women and that both women were in their third trimester of pregnancy. He was very frustrated because, in his words, "I do not want to be a father." He went on to explain that he could barely support himself and maintain his grades and that he had no one else supporting him. The young man further explained that he tried to encourage both women to terminate their pregnancy, but they both wanted to keep their babies. He felt defeated about the situation, but what he did not seem to understand was the correlation between his decision making and his current situation. Even more troubling for him was the fact that he had so much anger toward the mothers of his children. I expressed to him that it was understandable for him to be edgy about finding out he was going to be a father to two children. I emphasized to him the importance of stepping up to the plate and putting himself in a position to support his children. The children, I reminded him, were not responsible for the situations. I further added that it was his decision that put himself in this situation in the first place. This was a bittersweet lesson for him to learn. I would like to think the young man departed our conversation with a better understanding about the consequences that come as a result of our own choices and the need to accept responsibility for those choices, even when they put us in the kind of predicament he was in. We all must take responsibility for the choices we make, and sometimes the consequences of our choices can derail us from the path and plans we intended for ourselves. Unfortunately, I did not see the young man again following our conversation.

Students, it is very important that you concern yourselves with the consequences that come along with the decisions and choices you make, especially when it comes to matters that can greatly affect the plans you have laid out for yourself. Be mindful that unwanted pregnancy is not the only matter of concern for students when it comes to dating and the people you choose to spend your time with. Consider actions that can lead to consequences of contracting sexually transmitted diseases (STDs), which include HIV and AIDS.

When is sex consensual? Consent is another pressing issue that has become a growing concern on college campuses all across the U.S. The statistics are shocking as it relates to campus sexual assaults, violence and sex crimes. According to the National Violence Sexual Resource Center information and statistics for journalist; one in 5 women and one in 16 men are sexually assaulted while in college (i), even more staggering is that 90% of sexual assault victims on college campuses do not report the assault (c) . The report further states that rape is the most under-reported crime; 63% of sexual assaults are not reported to police (o).

Literary sources say sexual consent occurs when one person voluntarily agrees to the proposal or desires of another. The concept of consent has been enlisted to function in several major contexts, including in law, medicine and sexual relationships. Types of consent include: implied consent, informed consent, and unanimous consent. Consent as understood in legal contexts may differ from the everyday meaning. For example, a person under the age of sexual consent may willingly engage in a sexual act, but the consent is not valid in a legal context. Also be mindful that the age of consent may vary from state to state.

More and more we are hearing stories in the news of college drinking and behavior that is less than favorable. College drinking has become a ritual that many college students see as an integral part of the college experience. A surprising number of students report experiencing alcohol related sexual assault and date rape. For this very reason, young men and women are urged to take this issue seriously. I strongly advise you to engage in responsible behavior when socializing while out to have *a good time.*

Also, I cannot stress enough the importance of being informed about consent. Be wise and above all, consider your actions and the consequences when making the choice to engage in sexual interaction with another person that may, can and will impact you as a student and as a person. Furthermore, keep in mind that alcohol is not an excuse, alcohol is a substance that can cause intoxication also known as drunkenness, alcohol has an effect of euphoria and lowers social inhibition, alcohol can cause unintentional injury which includes motor vehicle accidents, alcohol can alter your behavior, and many students are assaulted as a result of someone else's behavior related to alcohol and or recreational drug use.

You are adults, and these are real adult conversations you must have with yourselves and your partners about matters that can impact your educations and lives.

The key to managing your social life and academics is having the right balance. Enjoy your college experience, certainly, but remember that too much of a good thing can be a bad thing.

>Social Media

Social media has revolutionized communication and the sharing of information and content. From the interesting filters we can place on our pictures to the Internet sensations created overnight, or the fact that you can brand and market your products to individuals locally and abroad without paying large amounts of money, social media is a game changer.

However, like all great things, there is potential for misuse. Keep in mind that much of what you do on social media is a direct reflection of you. Be conscious that potential employers browse databases and social media profiles and perform Google searches on individuals and candidates they consider for hire. Various social media platforms provide more information about us than most of us are cognizant of; you might be surprised at the things potential employers find that you may have forgotten about. In some cases, social media profiles can be just as telling as a résumé or cover letter.

This was very much the case during a recent NFL draft. One of the players—considered to be the number-one draft pick—lost millions of dollars and dropped significantly in the draft rounds after a video surfaced on social media of him smoking a bong using a mask. The player acknowledged that it was him in the video. He explained that the video was two years old, but the damage was done. Questions regarding his commitment, work ethic, and decision-making abilities caused him to go from the projected round one pick to actually being drafted thirteenth. Students, be cognizant of what you post on social media profiles, because what you post can impact you long term. Remember, even if you delete something you post, it never really goes away. Social media postings will always be housed on a server somewhere.

SUCCESSFUL PEOPLE KNOW THE IMPORTANCE OF DEFERRED GRATIFICATION

Activity: State your thoughts on the discussion in chapter 13.

_____

_____

_____

_____

_____

_____

_____

_____

_____

_____

_____

_____

_____

_____

_____

_____

_____

Chapter 14

Get Up, Get Out, and Do Something

Often students have the idea that when they get a college degree, their lives will change overnight. While obtaining a degree may indeed lay your educational foundation and make you a more marketable candidate for positions, degrees are not the differentiator they once were. More individuals than ever have a postsecondary education. Therefore, you have to have been strategic and consciously engaged throughout your career as a college student to make yourself a truly marketable candidate after graduation.

Many students work very hard throughout college and truly earn their degree with honors, but because they were not strategic throughout their educational experience, many are unemployed or underemployed upon graduation. Students in this type of predicament are typically those who do not get real hands-on job experiences (such as an internship) working in the real world in their field of study *before* graduation. Working at a retail store does not prepare one to work in the criminal justice field. Working at a day care center can't prepare one to work as a financial analyst at a bank. Working at a fast-food restaurant does not prepare an education major to be an educator. Though these jobs may help to fund your education while working your way through college, they do not equip students with real-world work experience in their field of study. Work experience in your area of study is almost as crucial as the degree you earn. This is why I recommend to students to complete internships, externships, and cooperative education opportunities pertaining to their major and area of study while they are in school. Students who participate and complete internships related to their major during undergrad and graduate school are in better position for opportunities that lead to employment immediately following graduation.

Professional Skill Set Evaluation

List some of your skills and areas you feel are strengths for your major/area of study.

_____

_____

_____

What do you feel you need to improve on as it relates to your major/area of study?

_____

_____

_____

What resources are available to address your areas of growth?

_____

_____

_____

How efficient can you be in your profession upon strengthening your growth areas?

_____

_____

_____

I understand that many of you may be working to pay your way through college and have a lot on your plate, but gaining real-world job experience in your field is a necessity. A great plan of action to incorporate an internship or externship with a busy schedule is to fit internships in during the summer months. I recommend this period because generally, students' schedules are lighter during the summer months. I also know of individuals who participated in short-term internships during major school breaks. Speak with your academic advisor and your department leaders for information and guidance regarding obtaining internship and externship opportunities.

It is also important to note that there are both paid and unpaid internships. Do not overlook unpaid internships; you cannot put a value on obtaining real-world work experience. Both paid and unpaid internships can lead to employment opportunities.

In addition to participating in internships to gain real-world work experience, being involved in certain activities and organizations can also make you more marketable. Do all you can to increase the likelihood of obtaining employment upon graduation. For example, I am a huge fan of Toastmasters (www.toastmasters.org), an international organization dedicated to developing and improving its members' communication and leadership skills. Toastmasters prepares individuals to take on leadership responsibilities and provides a "supportive and positive learning experience" through practice and feedback. The skills I learned in Toastmasters were instrumental in allowing me to develop personally into a confident public speaker, which propelled me to be the change agent I am today.

There are Toastmaster chapters throughout the world. Initially I was shocked at the fact that I was completely oblivious that such a beneficial organization existed, but I was glad someone told me about it. And I am pleased to be able to share the information with you.

After I located a chapter of Toastmasters I felt was best suited to support my ambitions to grow as a speaker and build my network, I joined and became a member. I was blown away at how much I learned at each meeting. I was astonished at the caliber of individuals with whom I was now building effective, professional relationships. There were members in the chapter who worked for the Centers for Disease Control (CDC), government entities, as well as business owners and entrepreneurs. I actually received my

first real speaking engagement through a member of my

Toastmasters chapter. It was not a paid engagement, but I had the

opportunity to speak to hundreds of people. The experience bolstered my confidence that I could actually be a public speaker. On that day, the concept of Mr.

- YOUR LIFE DOES NOT GET BETTER - BY CHANCE IT GETS BETTER BY CHANGE

Phillips the Change Agent was born. I believe in the benefits of

Toastmasters so much that I require all my students to attend at

least one meeting. Sometimes you may have to commute a little

distance to the chapter that meets your goals and expectations. I

recommend visiting several chapters before settling on joining any

one chapter. Be sure you choose a Toastmasters chapter that is the

best fit for you. Remember, you can add organizations such as

Toastmasters on your résumé or social media profiles as well. This

is a great networking opportunity.

Another great strategy to maximize your college degree is to

join professional organizations. There are professional

organizations for nearly every major and profession. Many

organizations offer membership discounts for students, as well as student discounts when attending conferences and workshops. Joining industry organizations allows you the opportunity to grow professionally. You will also receive newsletters, industry-specific magazines, and the opportunity to attend professional conferences.

Becoming a member of professional organizations also affords you the ability to network with successful individuals in your field of study. Networking with professionals allows you to meet potential mentors and may even assist with the possibility of obtaining internship opportunities that can lead to full-time employment. When you attend workshops, meetings, or conferences, don't be afraid to get out of your comfort zone and network. More often than not, professionals at these events will be interested in communicating with you. Remember, a five-minute conversation with the right person can save you five years. Lastly,

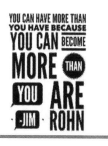

be sure to list all memberships of the various organizations on your résumé, cover letter, and professional social media platforms.

Activity: Get Up, Get Out, and Do Something

Conduct research and locate three professional organizations pertaining to your major. Write down their vision and mission statements.

_____

_____

_____

In what ways can you benefit professionally from joining the organizations you listed above? What about the personal benefits?

_____

_____

_____

What are the fees associated with joining the organizations? Does the organization offer discounts for college students?

_____

_____

_____

When is the organization's next interest meeting and/or conference? What, if any, fees are associated with attending?

_____

_____

_____

List information for the first meeting you will attend with a professional organization that pertains to your major.

Organization Name:_____

Address:_____

Phone:_____

Meeting Date and Time:_____

Related Fees/Parking:_____

(If possible, try to join at least one professional organization.)

Toastmasters

Visit www.toastmasters.org and browse through the website. What is the mission and vision of the organization?

_____

_____

_____

Use the search function on the Toastmasters website to locate and list three chapters that meet at locations and times convenient for you. Attend one meeting at each chapter.

_____

_____

_____

Summarize your experience at each Toastmasters meeting you attended. What did you enjoy? What did you dislike? What value (if any) do you see in the program? Would you consider joining?

_____

_____

_____

_____

_____

_____

_____

_____

_____

_____

_____

_____

Chapter 15

You'd Better Do Your Research

Recently, I read that the state of Texas is removing the requirement of a college degree to become a Child Protective Services caseworker. The article explained that the Texas Child Protective Services Department was taking drastic measures to increase the number of case managers because there was a large shortage of workers due to low salaries (ranging in the mid-thirties), which led to "staff shortages and turnover misfortunes." In many ways, this story emphasizes the importance of completing a career analysis before settling on a major. Unfortunately, many students do not conduct a career analysis at the right time, and as a result, do not have a full understanding of the requirements of the job, educational experiences necessary, or an understanding of the salary range for the career they intend to pursue.

Like so many other graduates after graduation, I was excited to begin living in my purpose, making an impact in my community, and earning a salary to support myself. But I soon discovered that because I had blindly selected a major based purely on passion, I found it challenging to make ends meet. Because those work experiences shaped the vast majority of the work that I do now, working with young adults, schools, colleges and parents, I do not regret the major I chose or my initial career path. I could have been much more strategic with my career path had I completed a more accurate and effective career analysis before I started my studies. While many professionals accept that it's not always about money, they are also cognizant that they cannot pay their bills with good intent and passion.

>Understanding Salary

Oftentimes when conducting research on potential salaries for various career choices, individuals tend to look at the highest income projections without an understanding that there are a variety of factors involved in determining compensation. Factors include experience, certifications, location, and the company itself. Furthermore, projections typically have outliers that are atypical of what one can really expect to earn. I will try to explain this concept without getting too mathematical. Generally, when looking at career income projections, you will encounter factors such as *mean* and *median*. The mean salary is the average salary for individuals in that particular profession. The challenge with only using the mean income when gauging one's potential salary is that a variety of outliers can distort the data.

Mean $10 + 8 + 4 = 22$ $22/3 = 7.3$	The average of the numbers: a calculated "central" value of a set of numbers.
Median 4, 8, 10 8 is the midpoint	A value or quantity lying at the midpoint of a frequency distribution of observed values or quantities.

For example: If there are six individuals whose salaries for a particular profession are as follows: $26,000, $28,000, $30,000, $31,000, $35,000, $37,000, the mean (average) salary is $31,166. However, if the sample set is expanded to include the income of one more person in the same field with a $70,000 salary, the mean jumps to $36,714, an increase of $6,000 over the average salary for the initial six salaries used in the calculation. Because the $70,000 salary is so much higher than the other salaries in the sample set and it causes the average to raise significantly, it is an outlier. When looking at mean projections, it is impossible to determine whether the figure includes or excludes outliers.

A better statistic to look at when comparing salary is the median. When we put the same salaries listed above in order from least to greatest, we can identify the median (middle) number as $31,000, a much more accurate potential salary indicator than the average salary of $36,714, which includes the outlier salary.

To accurately estimate potential salary, one must also take into account several other factors such as years of experience, education level, and certification status, as they all impact earning potential. Therefore, when conducting research on salary, available positions, and earning potential, one has to take into account the diversity of jobs within a given profession, the type of certifications that dictate earning potential, and the level of experience one has. Students cannot expect to graduate from college and earn what experienced certified individuals in the same profession earn. It is essential to conduct an honest assessment of your skill sets, experience, and educational level, so your salary estimates are as accurate as well as realistic.

The final components we will discuss in this chapter relating to salary are location and potential for growth within the profession. For instance, there are some professions projected to be obsolete in the next ten to fifteen years. Others are projected to grow extremely rapid. Examples of careers expected to have rapid growth include professions in the medical field, primarily because these services are needed by everyone. Because of aging baby boomers (an inundation of people born after World War Two), there is a huge need for individuals who can provide quality care in a variety of professions in the medical field. Information technology careers also continue be on the rise.

Another illustration of how projected growth impacts salary is the movie industry. The movie industry is growing rapidly in Atlanta, and there are not enough qualified individuals with skill sets in the film industry who reside in Atlanta to fill the positions. For that reason, individuals who obtain certifications in various fields related to the film industry such as film, editing, and videography have a good chance of obtaining gainful employment in Atlanta.

Now that you have a better understanding of how the projected growth and demand for a profession can impact salary and earning potential, let's talk further about how location may impact salary. Generally speaking, salaries are commensurate with cost of living. For example, the median salary for a given profession in New York is higher than the salary for the same profession in Georgia because the cost of living in New York is higher. Furthermore, the salary for an individual of a given profession employed in a rural location in Georgia is likely to be less than that for an individual of the same profession working in a major city in Georgia such as Atlanta, again because the cost of living is higher. The point here is that you must take into account several factors when gathering information about earning potential and determining if what you discover meets your expectations for your quality of life. Let's complete a couple of career projection activities.

Activity: Career Projection

"If you find your passion, you will never work another day in your life." Do you agree or disagree with this statement? Explain your response.

_____

_____

_____

Does your major and intended career path align with your passion? What degree is necessary to achieve your intended career path?

_____

_____

_____

What are the requirements necessary to pursue your intended career choice (e.g., education, certification, experience)?

_____

_____

_____

Upon graduation, what career path do you intend to pursue? Explain why you intend to pursue this path.

_____

How many of the requirements for your intended career path have you fulfilled?

If you are in the early stages of fulfilling your requirements, what are your plans and strategies to get it done?

Speak with the career services department at your school and perform a search with the United States Department of Labor (www.bls.gov), explore the Bureau of Labor Statistics (http://www.bls.gov/ooh/a-z-index.htm) and review the Occupational Outlook Handbook or similar entity to determine the mean and median salaries for the career you anticipate pursuing. Is this profession projected to grow over the course of the next ten to fifteen years?

_____

_____

_____

_____

_____

List three demographic areas you anticipate living upon graduation and write down the earning potential for each of those locations.

_____

_____

_____

Now that you have completed a basic career analysis, what are your thoughts regarding the career path you anticipate pursuing? Will you need to make any adjustments?

_____

_____

_____

_____

_____

_____

Chapter 16

The Credit Card Trap

Caution, new students! Beware of the easy CC, the credit card. Most college students can obtain a credit card quicker than some working adults. Before 2009, obtaining a credit card was made easy by vendors right on college campuses. The credit card companies were banking on you as a future wage earner. But the Card Act of 2009 changed this practice by limiting the ability of credit card companies to advertise credit cards on college campuses, and this reduced card issuances almost by half.

Students, I urge you to think twice! While credit cards are easy and quick to obtain, the debt can mount up even easier, leaving you with a monthly credit card expense that must be paid.

Visa, MasterCard, and Discover credit cards are some people's best friends. You see these logos on debit cards, prepaid cards, and even retail store credit cards. Due to the fact that it is not difficult to gain access to credit cards, every year credit card companies trap thousands of college students and adults in debt.

- Have you ever shopped at a retail store such as at Target,

Best Buy, or Macy's and been asked if you would like to apply for a store credit card?

• Have you ever received a notice in the mail stating that you have been preapproved for a credit card?

• Have you ever received a notice in the mail stating that you can transfer your balance on an existing credit card to a new credit card?

These are just a few ways people gain access to credit cards and get trapped into debt. Despite the fact that there is nothing wrong with having credit cards, you must be strategic when choosing and using your credit card to avoid being trapped in debt.

While there are dozens of best-practice strategies for how one can and should use credit to avoid being trapped in debt, we are going to focus on avoiding the most common traps and pitfalls that cause individuals to get entrapped in credit card debt.

You need to understand that credit card companies are in the business of making money, and they are willing to use all legal methods to do so. Lenders have many strategies to make

BETTER TO GO TO BED HUNGRY THEN TO WAKE UP IN DEBT

the largest profits possible. Some of the most common strategies they use are assessing cardholders the highest possible interest rates, charging late fees and penalties for late payments, and granting persons a large credit limit, even though they may not have earned it or met the income requirement. They often lure people in by offering deals such as no interest for a set period of time (usually six to twenty-four months), thereby encouraging cardholders to spend without thinking about the long-term consequence. Many credit card companies also offer deals that allow individuals to transfer their existing debt to a different credit card company. I, like many people, have experienced these traps. The significance here is to be informed about the practices credit card companies use. A few simple mistakes and mishandling of credit can take you years to repair. It can also cost you thousands in higher interest rates in the future when you apply for a car loan, a home loan, or any other type of loan.

Do not allow credit card debt to spiral out of control. Irresponsible credit card handling can ruin your credit before your life begins outside of college. Be vigilant; there is a whole new world awaiting you with the college experience. Be smart, wise, on the alert, frugal, and above all, guarded with your financial aid and any student loans you may need to take out for the necessity of your education.

>Interest Rate

One of the most important factors to focus on when considering a credit card or any loan with a lender is the interest rate they allocate you as the borrower. Interest is the proportion of a loan that is charged to the borrower. Basically the credit card companies and other lending institutes charge borrowers a fee for the use of the money they lend. The higher your interest rate and balance, the higher your overall payment is. The lower your interest rate and the less you borrow, the lower your payment will be. Interest rate in general is expressed as an annual percentage of the outstanding loan balance over a period of time, usually monthly. Your total payment is a combination of the principal (*the amount loaned*) and the interest charged.

How can you get the lowest possible interest rate? Your FICO score—an analysis of your debt-to-income (DTI) ratio, income, previous payment history, and several other factors—normally determines the interest rate you as a borrower will be given if you are issued credit. Credit scores range from 300 to 850; higher scores indicate that your debt represents less risk for the lender, so you will receive a lower interest rate. As a young college student, it is unlikely that you have had the opportunity to build good credit. At this point, you have what is called *building credit*. It is likely that you have yet to begin paying bills, have a car note, or acquired many of the types of creditworthy debt needed to help you build credit. Not having credit is not a bad thing; being in the credit-building stage is a better position than having bad or poor credit.

We will talk later in this chapter about how you can build your credit and maintain good credit.

As mentioned previously, the second component that determines your credit score is *debt-to-income ratio*, which simply means how much money you owe in comparison to how much money you make. Let's say you know someone who is in debt to a lot of people. Would you loan that person money? Chances are you would be hesitant because you would be concerned about their ability to pay you back. Credit card companies and lenders do the exact same thing. When lenders and credit card companies have concerns about your ability to pay them back, they either deny you the credit or approve you with a high interest rate, which means

you pay back much more than you borrowed. The key to avoid a

high DTI ratio is to try to maintain a low balance of debt. For

example, if you have a credit card with a $1,000 limit, you really

IT'S NOT ABOUT how much money YOU MAKE, ITS ABOUT HOW much you save

do not want to use more than about $300 of it, which means having an available balance of $700. Many people get trapped with a high DTI because they spend the entire credit

limit they were granted. This is known as maxing out the card, and

it's something you really should avoid doing. It hurts your credit

score and puts you in a financial strain. Also try to avoid having

too many credit cards or loans. Having ten credit cards with a

small balance of $300 each may not seem like much, but that adds

up to $3,000 of debt.

Additionally, I urge you to stay away from payday lenders,

rent-to-own contracts, and title loan companies (lenders who will

offer money when you use the title of your car as security). Many

consumers use these services to get a quick loan to buy items or

other immediate needs, but often the interest rates are extremely high and the business practices of these types of companies are questionable. For example, A title loan for $500 that is not paid back can cause an individual to have her car taken away and be left without transportation. The sad part about losing a car to a title loan of $500 is that, in most cases, the car is worth much more than $500. I really hope you can see that this type of company has no real incentive to work with you; they profit more when you default on the loan.

Recently, I saw an advertisement for a pay-as-you-go furniture company advertising a six-month lease special on a forty-inch television. It was valued at $179, with a biweekly lease payment of $29 (plus a hefty interest rate). This fee is ridiculous considering that TVs are very reasonably priced. By the time the lessee makes twelve $29 payments, they will have paid more than $400 for a $179 television. If, instead, you bought that same television at a retailer, you would own it immediately and for much less.

Living in the dorm can be an easy move. Some college students may choose to live off campus and share apartment housing; depending on the state, students may need to purchase large appliances such as a television, a refrigerator, and maybe a stove. But try to avoid using credit to purchase these items if possible. One great strategy to purchase larger items is to use layaway. Major store chains such as Sears, Wal-Mart, and many others have layaway plans that allow you to make a series of payments to purchase your items without having to use credit. So if you need a television, computer, refrigerator, dishes, or other items, layaway is a great way to eventually get what you need without using credit (particularly, if you can start your layaway order before you start college or move into your own apartment or dorm).

Another great strategy to purchase what you need without going into debt is to purchase pre-owned products, which will also save you money. Try using a classified advertising website such as Craigslist or similar platforms that will allow you to purchase used items for less. For example, I have firsthand knowledge of someone who purchased a four-year-old washer and dryer set for $250 on Craigslist. Being strategic and frugal is the name of the game to remain debt free.

>Making Payments on Credit Cards

One of the quickest ways to negatively impact your credit score and cause your interest rates to rise is to make late payments or not make your payments at all. When you make late payments or do not pay your debt, the lender will report your lack of payment to credit reporting agencies Equifax, Experian, and TransUnion. These negative marks of nonpayment will remain on your credit history for several months, and they will negatively impact your credit. Even if you pay your expenses on time for years and you miss one or two payments, your credit can still be negatively impacted. Cold world, right?

>Minimum Payments

All credit card statements inform you of your monthly minimum payment and due date. You should always pay the minimum payment on time, but I recommend that you pay more than the minimum payment so you can quickly pay off the debt and reduce the amount of interest you will owe. One of the best ways to ensure this happens is to plan ahead before you use your credit card.

For instance, a couple of years ago, I bought a MacBook Pro

laptop for about $2,000. I paid $500 cash and financed the remaining $1,500 on a credit card that allowed me to take advantage of the twenty-four months with no interest, meaning that if I paid the balance off before twenty-four months, I would only owe the actual amount I borrowed ($1,500). Before I actually purchased the computer, I did the math to figure out how much I needed to pay per month to make sure I paid off the laptop before the twenty-four month period. I decided to pay $100 each a month, which was higher than the $35 minimum payment required. Paying more than the minimum payment not only allowed me to pay off the debt in full by the twenty-four-month timeframe but also allowed me to pay it off sooner. This provided me with some flexibility. Having flexibility is important because things happen. There may have been a month when I could only pay the minimum payment, but paying more than the minimum payment due for prior months allowed me to stay ahead of the game. Try not to purchase items needed for college living without having a plan to pay them off in a reasonable amount of time, such as three to five months or sooner if possible. Always ask yourself before purchasing with your credit card these simple questions:

- "Is this a *want* or a *need*?"

- "Can I put this item on layaway?"

- "Can I pay cash for it?"

>Building Your Credit

As I mentioned earlier, it is very important to pay your debts on time. In addition to making payments on time, make every effort to reduce the number of credit inquiries into your credit report. You can do this by not applying for every credit card or store credit you are offered. Just because Best Buy, Macy's, or your favorite retailer offers you the chance to apply for a credit card, that does not mean you are obligated to accept the offer. Too many credit cards and too many inquiries can negatively impact your credit and credit score (FICO) and cause you to get into the credit card trap.

It is important to remember that many potential employers run credit and background reports, and having poor credit in some instances can impact your ability to obtain employment.

Let's talk about one of the easiest ways to build your credit: a secured credit card. Most banks and credit unions have the ability to issue secured credit cards. A secured credit card is a type of credit card that is made available to consumers who deposit funds into a security deposit account, which is held and used as collateral on the credit line available with the card. This means a required minimum amount of money is deposited with a financial institution into a security deposit account and held in the account in the event the cardholder does not make payment for the credit used for purchases. For example, to obtain a secured credit card for $300, you would be required to deposit $300 in a security deposit account. After using your secured credit card and making at least the minimum payments on time for several months, many banks and credit unions will convert your secured credit card to an unsecured credit card. This means you will no longer be required to maintain a security deposit account. Generally, when obtaining a secured credit card, the interest rate will be lower than applying for an unsecured credit card because the security deposit reduces the risk for the card issuer. As you make purchases using your secured credit card and make your minimum monthly payments, your payment history will be reported by the credit card issuer to the three major credit reporting agencies (Experian, Equifax, and TransUnion). Over the period of a few months, your credit history begins and your credit score will be calculated by FICO based on your usage and handling of your credit card. So make every effort to make your minimum payments on time. A plus with the secured credit card practice is that you may be able to obtain a secured credit card from multiple banking institutions, but be wise. I recommend using this strategy rather than acquiring credit cards with higher interest rates from retail stores and unsolicited preapproval notices you may receive in the mail.

>Credit Unions

Lastly, I recommend that students look into getting an account with a credit union. Credit unions tend to be more flexible to meet their members' banking needs and offer lower interest rates. Credit unions are a great option to obtain credit cards and other credit, but remember, whether you choose a traditional banking institution or a credit union, you must make your payments on time.

Activity: Credit Union Visit

Many large colleges have access to credit unions, and there are also a number of community credit unions that welcome new members. Visit a credit union and meet with a representative. Get the following questions answered:

What are the benefits of joining a credit union? What types of savings and checking accounts do they offer? What other services besides banking services do they offer members?

_____

_____

_____

What are the requirements to join the credit union?

_____

_____

_____

Does the credit union offer secured credit cards? Inquire about their process to obtain a secured credit card if you are interested.

_____

_____

_____

_____

If you decide to join the credit union, make an appointment to meet
with someone about savings and retirement. You are never too
young to start thinking about retirement! What did you learn?

_____

_____

_____

_____

_____

_____

_____

_____

_____

_____

_____

_____

_____

Activity: Debt Record

Name of Loan or Credit Card	Principal Owed	Interest Rate	Credit Limit Amount	Available Credit	Minimum Monthly Payment	Goal Monthly Payment (pay extra)
Total Debt Owed						

What do you notice about the amount of debt you owe in comparison to your credit limits? What is the ratio of total debt owed to your credit limit?

For example, if you owe an $800 debt and have a $1,000 credit limit, you have used 80 percent of your credit on this line. Which lenders/credit cards have high interest rates?

_____

_____

How does this impact what your goal monthly payment should be to pay off the balance sooner?

_____

_____

_____

View each lender's monthly statement. What types of purchases are impacting you the most (dining out, clothes, etc.)?

_____

_____

_____

_____

What changes regarding spending habits do you need to make (if any)?

_____

_____

_____

_____

Notes:_____

Chapter 17

When You Do More than What's Expected,

You Will Discover Your Gift

Many students graduate college with the expectation to *get a job*. But imagine how much more satisfying it would be to graduate college and *create a job*.

For years, I was not aware of this type of mindset. My whole life, I was taught to go to college, graduate, and get a good job. However, I eventually learned that for me to truly be happy, I needed to explore living in my purpose. For most of us who discover this, we cannot do this simply by working a nine-to-five job.

Please understand that I am not saying you should graduate and *not* have a goal of obtaining employment. What I am urging is that you have a plan as you prepare to graduate and obtain your first job. I want you to consider if that job will eventually help you fulfill your purpose.

I am often asked how I became Mr. Phillips the Change Agent, a speaker and an author. In general, I respond with an answer I think disappoints many (simply because they expect an overly complex response). The ventures I am involved in today as a change agent were jumpstarted by my participation as a mentor to a group of young men while serving as a middle school teacher. Our mentor group would meet on Saturdays, and we took field

 trips and participated in activities outside of school hours. As my team and I worked to develop activities to engage the young participants, I began creating educational hip-hop songs with the young men in the group to keep them motivated and interested in staying in school. Unfortunately, there was no budget for the program. Because my team leaders and I could see how the youths benefited from the mentoring program (and because we believed we were making a difference in these young men's lives and the community), we found ourselves funding the program out of our own pockets to make things happen for the mentor group. I did not get an award for serving with the mentor group; I did not expect to receive accolades for spearheading the program. My role of mentor was not listed in my job description. The point I am trying to make is that I found something I was passionate about while encouraging

young people to stay in school and work to reach their full potential. As a result of our hard work with the mentoring group, we were eventually recognized by a nationally known radio personality in Atlanta, and our kids were invited to the radio station to share our anti-bullying song.

It was through these ventures, working to motivate and inspire youths, that the birth of the Change Agent concept came about.

I have had the opportunity to speak to hundreds of middle and high school students as well as college students and a variety of other audiences throughout the country. It is through my efforts to inspire and motivate others to strive to reach their full potential that I found my passion. I came to appreciate that in addition to being a teacher, there is more to me. I was able to come to this realization because of one action: I chose to do more than what was expected of me, and in that effort, I discovered my passion.

Not everyone is destined to be a public speaker or an author, but I challenge you to seek out your passion and reach beyond simply being *content* with getting a job upon graduation. Take a moment to reflect back on this powerful quote when you feel yourself slipping into the habit of doing just enough to get by: "If you don't build your own dreams, someone else will hire you to help build theirs."—Tony Gaskins Jr.

As we wrap things up, keep in mind that you can become whatever you are willing to sacrifice and work for. At times, you may have to lose sleep, sacrifice some weekends, change your spending habits, or even find a new circle of influence. But trust me, it's all worth it.

Make a conscious effort to apply the principles in this book and be strategic throughout your college experience and beyond. Above all, be an intentional student, and you can achieve the ultimate college experience. You can reach your optimal level of academic performance.

Continue to be great, and I will see you at the top, because the bottom is too crowded.

College Glossary

Academic advisor: a member of a school's faculty who provides advice and guidance to students on academic matters such as course selections.

Academic year: the annual period during which a student attends and receives formal instruction at a college or university, typically from August or September to May or June. The academic year may be divided into semesters, trimesters, quarters, or other calendars.

Accredited: Having official recognition that a college or university meets the standards of a regional or national association. Although international students are not required to attend an accredited college or university in the United States, employers, other schools, and governments worldwide often only recognize degrees from accredited schools.

ACT (American College Test): a standardized college entrance exam administered by the American College Testing program. Four separate multiple-choice tests measure knowledge of English, math, reading, and science, and one optional writing test measures essay planning and writing skills.

Affidavit of support: an official document proving adequate funding from an individual or organization to cover an international student's educational and living expenses while enrolled at a United States college or university.

AP (Advanced Placement program): a program offered by the College Board, a US-based nonprofit educational organization that allows students to take college-level courses while in high school. Students can then take standardized AP exams; those with qualifying scores can earn credit at certain colleges and universities.

Assistantship: a financial aid award granted to a graduate student to help pay for tuition that is offered in return for certain services, such as serving as a teaching assistant or research assistant.

Associate's: an undergraduate degree awarded by a college or university upon successful completion of a program of study, usually requiring two years of full-time study. An associate's degree is typically awarded by community colleges; it may be a career or technical degree, or it may be a transfer degree, allowing students to transfer those credits to a four-year bachelor's-degree-granting school.

Bachelor's: an undergraduate degree awarded by a college or university upon successful completion of a program of study, typically requiring at least four years (or the equivalent) of full-time study.

College: a postsecondary institution that typically provides only an undergraduate education, but in some cases, also graduate degrees. The terms *college, university,* and *school* are often used interchangeably. Separately, *college* can also refer to an academic division of a university, such as a college of business

Core requirements: mandatory courses that students are required to complete to earn a degree.

Course: a regularly scheduled class on a particular subject. Each college or university offers degree programs that consist of a specific number of required and elective courses.

Course load: the number of courses or credits a student takes during a specific term.

Credits: units that a school uses to indicate that a student has completed and passed courses required for a degree. Each school defines the total number and types of credits necessary for degree completion, with every course being assigned a value in terms of credits, credit hours, or units.

Dean: the head of a division of a college or university.

Degree: a diploma or title awarded to students by a college or university after successful completion of a program of study.

Discipline: an area of academic study.

Dissertation: an in-depth, formal writing requirement on an original topic of research that is typically submitted in the final stages before earning a doctorate (PhD).

Dormitories or Dorms: student housing provided by a college or university. These accommodations are also known as residence halls and feature living quarters, bathrooms, common areas, and possibly a kitchen or cafeteria.

Drop: to withdraw from a course. A college or university typically has a period of time at the beginning of a term during which students can add or drop courses.

Electives: courses that students can choose to take for credit toward a degree, but are not required.

ESL (English as a second language): a course or program of study used to teach English to nonnative English speakers.

Enroll: to register or enter a school or course as a participant.

Extracurricular activities: optional activities, such as sports, that students can participate in outside of academic classes.

Faculty: a school's teaching and administrative staff; members of the faculty are also often responsible for designing programs of study.

FAFSA (Free Application for Federal Student Aid): application used by US citizens and permanent residents to apply for financial aid from US federal and state governments.

Fees: an amount of money charged by colleges and universities (in addition to tuition) to cover costs of services such as libraries and computer technology.

Financial aid: all types of money offered to a student to help pay tuition, fees, and other educational expenses. This can include loans, grants, scholarships, assistantships, fellowships, and work-study jobs.

Fraternity: a student organization, typically for men, formed for social, academic, community service, or professional purposes.

Freshman: a student in the first year of high school or college/university.

GMAT (Graduate Management Admission Test): a standardized graduate business school entrance exam administered by the nonprofit Graduate Management Admission Council. The GMAT measures verbal, quantitative, and analytical writing skills. Some business schools accept either the GMAT or GRE.

GPA (grade point average): a student's overall academic performance, which is calculated as a numerical average of grades earned in all courses. The GPA is determined after each term, typically on a 4.0 scale, and upon graduation, students receive an overall GPA for their studies.

Graduate school: the division of a college or university, or an independent postsecondary institution, which administers graduate studies and awards master's degrees, doctorates, or graduate certificates.

Grant: a type of financial aid that consists of an amount of free money given to a student, often by the federal or a state government, a company, a school, or a charity. A grant does not have to be repaid. The term *grant* is often used interchangeably with *scholarship*.

GRE (Graduate Record Examination): a standardized graduate school entrance exam administered by the nonprofit Educational Testing Service (ETS), which measures verbal, quantitative, and analytical writing skills. The exam is generally required by graduate schools.

Independent study: an academic course that allows students to earn credit for work done outside of the normal classroom setting. The reading or research assignment is usually designed by the students themselves or with the help of a faculty member, who monitors the progress.

IRS (Internal Revenue Service): the US government agency that collects income taxes. International students who work on or off campus or receive taxable scholarships must pay taxes.

Internship: an experience that allows students to work in a professional environment to gain training and skills. Internships may be paid or unpaid and can be of varying lengths during or after the academic year.

Ivy League: an association of eight private universities located in the Northeastern United States, originally formed as an athletic conference. Today, the term is associated with universities that are considered highly competitive and prestigious. They include: Brown University, Columbia University, Cornell University, Dartmouth College, Harvard University, the University of Pennsylvania, Princeton University, and Yale University.

Junior: a student in the third year of high school or college/university.

Junior college: a two-year postsecondary institution that offers the associate's degree.

Letter of recommendation: a letter written by a student's teacher, counselor, coach, or mentor that assesses his or her qualifications and skills.

Liberal arts: academic studies of subjects in the humanities, social sciences, and the sciences with a focus on general knowledge, in contrast to a professional or technical emphasis. The term *liberal arts* is often used interchangeably with *liberal arts and sciences* or *arts and sciences.*

Liberal arts college: a postsecondary institution that emphasizes an undergraduate education in liberal arts. The majority of liberal arts colleges have small student bodies, do not offer graduate studies, and focus on faculty teaching rather than research.

Loan: a type of financial aid that consists of an amount of money that is given to someone for a period of time, with an agreement that it will be repaid later, usually with interest.

Major: the academic subject area that a student chooses to focus on during his or her undergraduate studies. Students typically must officially choose their major by the end of their sophomore year, allowing them to take a number of courses in the chosen area during their junior and senior years.

Matriculate: to enroll in a program of study at a college or university with the intention of earning a degree.

MBA: a master of business administration degree.

Midterm exam: an exam given after half of the academic term has passed that covers all material studied in a particular course until that point. Not all courses have midterm exams.

Minor: an academic subject area that a student chooses to have a secondary focus on during undergraduate studies. Unlike a major, a minor is typically not required, but it allows a student to take a few additional courses in a subject different from his or her major.

Need-based financial aid: financial aid that is awarded to students due to their financial inability to pay the full cost of attending a specific college or university, rather than specifically because of their grades or other merit.

Net price calculator: an online tool that allows students and families to calculate a personalized estimate of the cost of a specific college or university, after taking into account any scholarships or need-based financial aid that an applicant would receive.

Nonresident: a student who does not meet a state's residence requirements. A college or university may have different tuition costs and admissions policies for residents versus nonresidents. In most cases, international students are considered nonresidents.

Open admissions: a college or university's policy of accepting all students who have completed high school, regardless of their grades or test scores, until all spaces are filled. Most community colleges have an open admissions policy, including for international students.

Orientation: a college or university's official process of welcoming new, accepted students to campus and providing them with information and policies before classes begin, usually in a half-day or full-day event.

Part-time student: a student who is enrolled at a college or university but is not taking the minimum number of credits required for a full course load.

Pass/fail: a grading system in which students receive either a passing or failing grade, rather than a specific score or letter grade. Certain college or university courses can be taken pass/fail, but these typically don't include ones taken to fulfill major or minor requirements.

Plagiarism: the use of another person's words or ideas as your own, without acknowledgment of the original source. Schools have different policies and punishments for students caught plagiarizing, which tends to occur with research papers and other written assignments.

Prerequisite: a required course that must be completed before a student is allowed to enroll in a more advanced one.

Priority date: the date by which an application must be received in order to be given full consideration. This can apply to admissions, financial aid, and on-campus housing. After the priority date passes, applications may be considered on a case-by-case or first-come, first-served basis.

Probation: a status or period of time in which students with very low GPAs (or whose academic work is otherwise unsatisfactory according to the school) must improve their performance. If they are unable to do so, they may be dismissed from the school.

Provost: the senior academic officer of a college or university who typically oversees all academic policies and curriculum-related matters.

Quarters: periods of study that divide the academic year into four equal segments of approximately twelve weeks each, typically including the summer.

Registrar: the college or university official who is responsible for registering students and keeping their academic records, such as transcripts.

Registration: the process in which students choose and enroll in courses to be taken during the academic year or in summer sessions.

RA (Resident assistant): a student leader who works in campus dormitories and supervises issues and activities related to dorm life.

Rolling admissions: an admissions process used by some colleges and universities in which each application is considered as soon as all the required materials have been received, rather than by a specific deadline. Colleges and universities with this policy will make decisions as applications are received until all spaces are filled.

Room and board: housing and meals. Room and board is typically one of the costs that colleges and universities will list in their annual estimated cost of attendance, in addition to tuition, fees, and textbooks and supplies. If students choose to live in dormitories, they may be required to buy into a meal plan to use on-campus dining facilities.

SAT (Scholastic Aptitude Test): a standardized college entrance exam administered by Educational Testing Service (ETS) on behalf of the nonprofit college board, which measures reading, writing, and math skills. Most students take the SAT during their junior or senior year of high school, and most colleges and universities accept either SAT or ACT scores.

Scholarship: a type of financial aid that consists of an amount of free money given to a student by a school, individual, organization, company, charity, or federal or state government. The term *scholarship* is often used interchangeably with *grant*.

Semesters: periods of study that divide the academic year into two equal segments of approximately fifteen to eighteen weeks each.

Seminar: a course offered to a small group of students who meet with a professor to discuss specialized topics.

Senior: a student in the fourth year of high school or college/university.

Social Security number: a nine-digit number issued by the US government to people who are authorized to work in the United States and collect certain government benefits.

Sophomore: a student in the second year of high school or college university.

Sorority: a student organization for women formed for social, academic, community service, or professional purposes. Like a fraternity, a sorority is part of a college or university's Greek system.

Standardized tests: exams (such as the SAT, ACT, and GRE) to measure knowledge and skills. Standardized tests are designed to be consistent in how they are administered and scored. Standardized tests are intended to help admissions officials compare students who come from different backgrounds.

TA (teaching assistant): a graduate student who assists a professor with teaching an undergraduate course, usually within his or her field, as part of an assistantship.

Tenure: a status offered to high-level faculty members at a college or university that allows them to stay permanently in their positions, after demonstrating a strong record of teaching and published research.

Term: a period of study, which can include semesters, quarters, trimesters, or summer sessions.

Thesis: a formal piece of writing on a specific subject, which may be required to earn a bachelor's or master's degree.

Transcript: an official record of a student's coursework and grades at a high school, college, or university. A high school transcript is usually one of the required components of the college application process.

Transfer credit: credit granted toward a degree on the basis of studies completed at another college or university. For instance, students who transfer from a community college to a four-year college may earn some transfer credit.

Tuition: an amount of money charged by a school per term, per course, or per credit, in exchange for instruction and training. Tuition generally does not include the cost of textbooks, room and board, and other fees.

Undergraduate student: a student enrolled in a two-year or four-year study program at a college or university after graduation from high school.

Undergraduate studies: a two-year or four-year study program at a college or university leading to an associate's or bachelor's degree.

University: a postsecondary institution that typically offers both undergraduate and graduate degree programs. The term *university* is often used interchangeably with *college* and *school*.

Withdraw: to formally stop participating in a course or attending a university.

Work/Study: a financial aid program funded by the US federal government that allows undergraduate or graduate students to work part time on campus or with approved off-campus employers. To participate in work study, students must complete the FASFA.

~ ~ ~

* Glossary Information retrieved from
http://www.usnews.com/education/best-colleges/articles/2011/08/15/us-higher-education-glossary

Electronic Catalogue

Accessed (2016). ncjrs.gov
(i)Krebs, C. P., Lindquist, C., Warner, T., Fisher, B., & Martin, S. (2007). The campus sexual assault (CSA) study: Final report. Retrieved from the National Criminal Justice Reference Service: http://www.ncjrs.gov/pdffiles1/nij/grants/221153.pdf

Accessed (2016). ncjrs.gov
(c) Fisher, B., Cullen, F., & Turner, M. (2000). The sexual victimization of college women (NCJ 182369). Retrieved from the National Criminal Justice Reference Service: https://www.ncjrs.gov/pdffiles1/nij/182369.pdf

Accessed (2016). bjs.ojp. usdoj.gov
(o) Rennison, C. A. (2002). Rape and sexual assault: Reporting to police and medical attention, 1992-2000 [NCJ 194530]. Retrieved from the U.S. Department of Justice, Office of Justice Programs, Bureau of Justice Statistics: http://bjs.ojp.usdoj.gov/content/pub/pdf/rsarp00.pdf

Phillips, P. L. (2015). Educational Empowerment Group, LLC. Text Picture Art: Application used: WordSwag.

Accessed (2016). Bureau of Labor Statistics: Occupational Outlook Handbook (bls.gov) www.bls.gov/ooh/a-z-index.htm

Retrieved (2016). College Glossary: usnews.com/education/best-colleges/articles/2011/08/15/us-higher-education-glossary

Connect With Us

www.MrPhillipsTheChangeAgent.com

 @MrPhillipsTheChangeAgent

 @MrPhillipsTheChangeAgent

 @ChangeAgent1

 @MrPhillipsTheChangeAgent

ABOUT THE AUTHOR

Patrick Phillips, "The Change Agent," is a doctoral student, college instructor, urban education specialist, inspirational speaker, certified educator, and school social worker. He is a recipient of the President of the United States Volunteer Service Award and the author of *Decisions: A Young Man's Guide to Avoiding the Traps*, *Change 101: Average Is Crowded*, and the *Decisions: Success Is Optional* curriculum. Mr. Phillips is a graduate of Georgia State University (GSU). He holds master's and bachelor's degrees in social work.

He was raised in a single-parent household in South Central Los Angeles and overcame many of the challenges that youth, young adults, and adults face today. He has an extensive background in working with youth, families, adults, community organizations, and college students. He uses his experiences to educate, empower, and help others achieve self-actualization.

Mr. Phillips is a board member with Fulton County's My Brother's Keeper and the 500 Men Standing in the GAP taskforces. He has partnered with various organizations, schools, and colleges throughout the United States. Mr. Phillips has spoken to thousands of youth, parents, and community stakeholders. Additionally, Patrick's motivational/educational videos and audio tapes, which have nearly 200,000 views and listens on YouTube and various social media platforms, have been played in classrooms and for organizations throughout the United States. He continues to facilitate change one engagement at a time. You can gain access to his educational materials at www.mrphillipsthechangeagent.com.

41200299R00117

Made in the USA
Middletown, DE
06 March 2017